D1029981

The British Theatre

The British Theatre

ALEC CLUNES

CASSELL · LONDON

Cassell & Company Limited
35 Red Lion Square · London WC1

and at

MELBOURNE · SYDNEY · TORONTO
JOHANNESBURG · CAPE TOWN · AUCKLAND

Made and printed in Great Britain by
William Clowes and Sons, Limited, London and Beccles
F.1263

Acknowledgements

The publishers of this volume are grateful to the following for permission to include extracts from the undermentioned books:

The Public Trustee (Executors for the Estate of Bernard Shaw) and The Society of Authors for *The Quintessence of Ibsenism* and *Dramatic Opinions and Essays*.
Secker and Warburg Ltd. for *The Irresistible Theatre* by W. Bridges-Adams.
Rupert Hart-Davis Ltd. and Mrs Eva Reichmann for *Around Theatres* by Max Beerbohm.

Contents

CHAPTER ONE

Early Theatre

In the beginning was not the word but the grunt and the gesture. Then came the spoken word; then writing, first carved on stone, then written on parchment, then printed on paper. Some three and a half thousand years separate Shakespeare's first play from the first written play, carved on Egyptian stone. But history is as much a process of deduction as of assembling material records, and we may guess with some precision what form drama-before-writing took from an examination of the dramatic rituals extant among contemporary primitive tribes isolated from civilization and the pressures of the printed word.

A birth, a mating or a death; drought or flood; the departure or return of the hunters; seed-time and harvest; war with bad neighbours or peace with good; the building of a new shelter against the elements; each brought an imperative, corporate need to ask or give thanks. A costume, perhaps a mask; a chant; and a dance; a ritual to be repeated in which the leaders led, the less power-loving responded, and all forgot themselves in festivity. Theatre and religion were born in the same moment—and of the same need. Actor and witch-doctor were one; and still are. Story-tellers.

Egypt Amongst the earliest writings yet discovered are those that come from Egypt; they are, for the most part, religious in character. When a great king died thousands of people were put to work building his tomb. When he was buried he was surrounded by all the things in life that he had held most dear and by all that the priests could imagine would assist him on his voyage through the after-life. Carved on the walls of the insides of the tombs were prayers and other religious writings. The tombs were sealed and many did not see the light of day again until some three or four thousand years had passed. It is to one of these tombs that we owe our knowledge of the first written play.

There is in the British Museum a stone which was found among the Egyptian tombs.

1

(Cave-drawing of man in animal-skin) **The Earliest theatrical document extant**

15,000 to 25,000 years ago, primitive man recorded in cave-drawings (*a*) the technique of hunting by lure, (*b*) an act of religious worship and (*c*) a feat of mimicry. It seems reasonable to assume that the better the mimicry, the more successful the hunting—and the more powerful the priest. The drawing (retouched) is from the Cave of the Three Brothers in the French Pyrenees, discovered in 1914. Primitive tribes still hunt, worship and perform in the same way—and more civilized peoples still feel the need to blend (and confuse) religious ritual, pantomime and survival techniques. Likewise the drawing could easily be mistaken for the work of a way-out contemporary

**(Temple Model)
Earliest civilized
theatre**

Isolated tribal living gave place to organized city life, primitive man became civilized man, power passed from the local witch-doctor, or medicine-man, to kings ruling over mighty empires. Man felt compelled to think of kings as gods and built massive temples in which to bury them. In front of such temples, priest-actors recalled the god-king's power and virtues by performing play-stories of their lives. The temples no longer exist but this photograph of a reconstructed model of the Temple at Deir El-Bahri by the banks of the Nile, gives a reasonable impression of the grandeur of the setting in which took place the performance of the Egyptian 'Passion' plays described in the text. (*Copyright Metropolitan Museum, New York*)

**(Priests in Animal-mask) Egyptian
priest-actors**

The priests' continuing reliance on animal masks to add to their stature and dominance is made evident by this detail showing the construction of priests' masks. (*Copyright Mariette-Bey, Dendérah*)

Scholars date it at about 2000 B.C., and many think that this is a copy of an older document of about 3400 B.C. The carving on this stone is thought to be a play—it is in dialogue form and contains stage directions. It is assumed that the actors were priests and that their performance was given in memory of a dead king. A tax was levied on the town to finance the performance. The plot of the play deals with the journey of the soul of the dead king, until he becomes one of the Imperishable Stars, and with his resurrection.

Plays similar to this were performed throughout Egypt until three hundred or four hundred years after the birth of Christ. Then Christianity became the official religion in Egypt and the place where the old plays had been acted for some three thousand five hundred years or more was burnt.

Greek Theatre Some two thousand five hundred years ago Athens was the centre of the civilized world. Here the tragic and comic theatre as we know them were born and grew up as part of the greatest experiment in social organization that the world has known. Democracy, the rule of the people, may remain an ideal yet to be realized; but Athenian democracy, with all its imperfections, set a standard against which successive civilizations have measured their failures. In this astonishing community, philosophy, politics, art and religion lived side by side in amity, not warring across in-valid frontiers but seeking to find a dignity in man's dealings with man.

The day of all days in the Athenian year was spent in the theatre. It was a state occasion of the utmost civic and national importance, calling not only for splendour and solemnity but for much revelling. Above all, it was a religious occasion—but with a difference. For the god to whom the people drank and gave thanks was a companionable god, a jolly giant only a little over life-size. Dionysus, the god of wine and fertility, was himself given to the most prodigious pranks, and as his religion was enviably innocent of admonition, his springtime festival celebrated the intoxicating miracle of life with appropriate exuberance. The city and its many visitors assembled at the huge open-air theatre for the preface to five or six days of celebration. Carved out of the hillside was the sweeping semi-circle of tier upon tier of seats and here were seated some sixteen thousand people, with as many more perched high on the surrounding hillside. Dressed in their gayest colours (for

(Greek Animal-masks) **Greek animal masks and costumes**

The illustration is from a drawing on a vase and shows the actors in a comus. The comus was the lay comic afterpiece that followed the religious tragedies in the early Greek drama festivals—and later became the nursery of satire and of plays about people rather than gods. (*Copyright Lionel D. Barnett*)

Evolution of the Greek theatre building As speech begins to conquer spectacle, the dancing circle gives place to the semi-circular acting arena backed by imposing buildings

(1) EPIDAURUS. Here can still be seen the earlier type of Greek theatre. The original Theatre of Dionysus at Athens is thought to have had a very similar circular arena. (*Copyright Allardyce Nicoll*)

(2) THE THEATRE OF DIONYSUS AT ATHENS as it now remains illustrates a later form of Greek theatre. The arena has become semi-circular, and behind the actors impressive buildings will rise to take the place of a clear vista of countryside and sky. (*Copyright Mansell Collection*)

(3) From such ruins as are extant it is possible to conjecture what the appearance of the Athens Theatre of Dionysus must have been like during its hey-day in the fifth century B.C. One such reconstruction, depicting a performance of Aeschylus's *Agamemnon*, is the work of Heinrich Bulle under the direction of Franz Rapp. (*Copyright Mrs Franz Rapp*)

Greek tragedy

The richness and beauty of the stage-costumes used in Greek tragedy is well suggested by this illustration of Andromeda drawn from an Attic vase. (*Copyright Allardyce Nicoll*)

Greek comedy

From a vase of the fifth century B.C. comes a satiric burlesque of a love scene famous in Greek mythology, featuring Mercury, Jupiter and Alcmena. (*Copyright Princeton University Press*)

Sunday best was never Sunday drab) peasants from the remotest villages of Attica rubbed shoulders and shared their wine-skins with the townsmen—even the city gaols released their prisoners. For months past the authorities had been preparing for the occasion. Dramatists from all over the country submitted new plays based on old stories of the gods and the three best were chosen and performed in competition. As the names were announced, the dramatists, with their 'backers' and actors, paraded in the richest of robes and were crowned so that all might know and honour them.

The statue of Dionysus was borne out into the country and set on its pedestal under an olive-tree while the ritual sacrifice was made; after which everyone took part in games, feasting and improvised revelry. As night fell, all returned (carrying the wine high overhead in beautiful jars, garlanded with fresh flowers) joining in a torchlight procession back to the theatre, where the god was enthroned beside his stage. Here, in the following days, the dramatic contest took place. No charge was made for admission—a rich citizen assisted the State to pay all the expenses. He was chosen by lot—as were the leading actors. The dramatists, who were all actors, directed their own plays, designed the costumes, composed the music and dances and trained the chorus.

At dawn the next morning the whole theatre and the surrounding hillside was bustling with people; the city fathers, the important visitors and the Priest of Dionysus taking the seats of honour. The sun rose, a herald commanded attention, and the vast concourse hushed as a group of fifty white-robed figures entered the stage—a full circle, 64 ft. across. The chorus chanted in unison, then a single voice answered them—a god-like figure,

6

dressed in magnificent robes, standing head and shoulders above all others. The story they told was epic in mood—gods and heroes involved in heroic labours and tragic catastrophes—and the audience's pleasure came not from any suspense as to the outcome but from the dramatist's power to wring tragic irony from a familiar story. Later in the morning, there followed a Satyr-play, in which the tragic story was re-told in terms of burlesque, a crude farce. The rough-and-tumble antics of the Satyrs—hairy clowns, horned and tailed—presented a devil's-eye view. Later in the day, there followed yet another play, a topical comedy, lampooning familiar notables and events of the day in a riotous jumble of savage caricature, dirty jokes, topical gags, animal impersonations and clowning. The next two days followed the same pattern and, after a further day or two of competitions between rival choruses, singers and actors, the judges (a special jury—one from each of the ten tribes of Attica—chosen by lot and sworn to impartiality) gave their decision. The victorious dramatist and his backer were crowned and that night were the centre of a great banquet given in their honour. They were the men of the day. And this day had been the day of all days in the Athenian year.

The theatre may not have been born with the Greeks but the Greeks gave order to an astonishing variety of major theatrical developments:

1. The first civic buildings solely devoted to dramatic performances.
2. The first plays written not by priests but by poets of the people.
3. The first secular plays on domestic and topical subjects.
4. The first state-supported guilds of actors.
5. The first painted scenery and mechanical stage-effects.
6. The first theatrical costumes, neither historical nor contemporary but elaborating a convention of their own.
7. The first dramatic contests.

Early Theatre

This is a picture of the Greek theatre in its high days. Like democracy, it had evolved from humbler beginnings, many of which we know only from conjecture. And, like democracy, it was to dwindle, die and be born again in a multiplicity of varying forms. But never in any succeeding civilization have the people and the state, the drama and religion shared so equally such a close and joyously elevating experience.

Greek Theatre—A Brief History The first dramatic contest was won by Thespis, in 534 B.C. Hitherto the plays had been recited by a chorus and the chorus leader but Thespis added the first actor, thus making duologue possible. Stories recollected in song and chant gave place to stories demonstrated in action; past tense became present tension. Thespis, remembered as the first actor, introduced the mask and make-up, permitting characterization; he is also the first recorded impersonator of women—there were no actresses.

Some fifty years later Aeschylus won the contest for the first time. He had introduced a second actor, permitting further elaboration of action. He is remembered as the first dramatist and seven of his seventy-odd plays are extant, the last of which—the *Oresteia*—abides as a world masterpiece. He also introduced stage costume, painted scenes and mechanical stage effects.

7

Seventeen years later, Sophocles, at the age of twenty-eight, triumphed over Aeschylus in the contest, which he was to win eighteen times. He introduced the third actor and subdued the role of the chorus. For some sixty years, in times of security and expansion, he wrote plays which brought the lives of the gods nearer to those of men; and was twice awarded the highest of state honours, the office of general. Seven of over one hundred plays are extant, the most famous of which—*Oedipus Rex*—was acclaimed by Aristotle as a model tragedy.

Forty years after Sophocles first won the contest, the prize went to Euripides, one of only four or five times it was to do so in over ninety attempts. Eighteen of his plays survive. In them the importance of the chorus continues to diminish (later it was to serve as mere entr'acte and finally to vanish altogether). The more conservative Sophocles said: 'I drew men as they ought to be—Euripides drew them as they are.' It was also said that people praised Aeschylus but read Euripides. Aeschylus had been a religious moralist and Sophocles an idealist; Euripides was a humanitarian reformer. Of humble birth, he was one of a growing body of sceptics who questioned, first, the authority of the gods—and then of the State and all conservative opinion. In *Ion* he portrayed a god, Apollo, who could lie and cheat—and showed that the Delphic oracle spoke with a voice more human than divine. In *The Trojan Women*, war was indicted for its horrors, not extolled for its heroics. In the *Medea* and *Hippolytus* he found vivid sympathy for the unjustly subjugated status in society of women. In *Andromache* he castigated those who held men as slaves. Play after play brought storm after storm to the placid calm of the contests. Traditionalism, finally stung to action, sent Euripides to exile. Soon after his death, his plays became prescribed reading for the schools. They were revived, not only in Greece but over the whole of the ancient world.

Aristophanes, the greatest of the writers of Old Comedy, presented *Lysistrata* at the contest some seventeen years later. This pacifist comedy of women who impose peace on their warring menfolk by banishing them from board and bed, is still performed to this day. Of his forty plays, seven are extant. Athens, during his life, was on the wane, its freedom threatened by constant wars and the subversion of democratic power by the tyrant, Cleon. Euripides had called men forward to extend their democracy. In changing times of insecurity, Aristophanes called them back to the old traditional virtues. As Athens went into decline, direct political attack became dangerous and the dramatists were driven to allegory and Utopian fantasies, and later turned to the more domestic comedy of manners.

In the eighty years that intervened before the arrival of the New Comedy, the theatre withdrew from the arena it had shared with religion and the State. Gone was the worship of heroes and gods, for heroes died and gods never lived. Gone was the pursuit of the ideal, for the ideal was unattainable. The glories of Greece had proved to be transitory— men were thrown back upon themselves. Menander, the Greek poet, showed them themselves in honest comedies of domestic and familiar events. He greatly extended the technical form of drama, formal duologue giving place to animated dialogue, familiar legends to realistic stories of surprise and suspense. He gave his audience neither what the priests wanted, nor what the philosophers wanted, nor what the social reformers wanted. He gave them what *they* wanted—portraits of themselves, recognizable as real, free from illusion. 'What was' was a thing of the past; 'What could be' was left to the future: all that mattered was 'what is'. How many of his hearers missed the pricking of the old spurs?

The Theatre of Rome The fastidious Greeks had forbidden any scene of violence on the stage—murders took place out of sight and were reported by messengers. The Romans were not so cissy. The world they now ruled had been conquered by ruthlessness; and the mammoth spectacles with which they celebrated each new conquest (and sought to keep their populace tame) were equally ruthless. Rome was all for reality and what Greeks had forbidden even in mimicry, Romans encouraged in actuality. Catullus wrote a mime of the crucifixion of a slave—occasionally it was acted by a real criminal who died a real death in agony on the cross. You can't get any more real than that. You can only get more lavish.

Do the signs of unrest seem to indicate that civil war is imminent, that all is not well here at the heart of the Roman Empire? The populace is unsettled. Rome is a babbling Babel, a city of many tongues, legion upon legion of slaves sent by conquering soldiers from all corners of the known world. A desperate government, in which the voices of many scrambling opportunists speak louder than the few patricians who have not gone a-colonizing, ponders how to distract its polyglot plebeians. Something is needed that will surmount the barriers of diverse languages and talk to the eyes, a mighty demonstration that will unite and lull into contentment the raggle-taggle mob that haunt the streets so

Early Theatre

Roman spectacle

Roman amphitheatres were built (or adapted) as Naumachia, or theatres for mimic sea-fights. There is a theory that even the dignity of the Athenian Theatre of Dionysus was desecrated by such barbaric spectacles, a Roman Emperor rendering it water-tight for such purposes. (*Copyright E. M. Laumann, La Machinerieau Théatre*)

9

threateningly. Seventy-four days in each year there will be chariot races; one hundred and one days in each year there will be dramatic performances (nearly half the year given up to public holiday). A horde of contractors are paid out of public funds to devise mimic spectacles to impress a mob already glutted by constant real spectacles, streets stuffed with squadron upon squadron of conquerors returning at the head of glorious processions of captive kings and their exotic peoples, the soldier's rich bag of human loot.

Mammoth audiences watched mammoth spectacles. 'What pleasure is there in seeing 600 mules in the *Clytemnestra*, or 3,000 bowls in the *Trojan Horse*?' Cicero might have saved his breath; this was no time for captious dramatic criticism. Plays, dramatists and actors alike were swamped by ever more lavish and dazzling spectacles. Hordes of wild beasts were starved to frenzied hunger and put into giant arenas with slaves and robbers. The protagonists present, the play was left to construct itself, the actors to extemporize their short scene of suspense, their frantic delaying of the inevitable denouement. Huge new theatres were built to house great mimic battles, whole arenas were flooded to float great mimic sea-fights. The play was over only when one side was dead; and when the water was let out, any actors too damp for easy drying, thus expendable, were thrown to the animals. Life was cheap. What a show!

You would have thought such might was bound to be right. But when the invaders came, a long over-fleshed Rome fell with less spirit than many a Christian had shown in

the arenas. . . . What has the huge sweep of Rome up to power and down to decay left for us to remember of its theatre?

Its dramatic literature is negligible, mostly derivative, borrowing from the Greeks but debasing rather than refining. Nero's tutor, Seneca, in the intervals of trying to stop the

Roman tragedy

The tragic mask has just been placed on the table and the actor, his hair still ruffled, takes a rest. From a Roman fresco now in the Naples Museum. (*Copyright National Museum, Naples*)

10

big boy murdering his mother, wrote plays which, though more at home in the study than on the stage, nevertheless later exercised considerable influence on the French classical tragedies of Corneille and Racine. With Seneca's death, written drama virtually ceased, giving way to mimic spectacles and the more extempore popular 'plays of low life' written with such savage satire that the authorities found it necessary to destroy theatres in the city and forbid performances within one mile of the city gates. For the rest it is a tale of actors rather than of writers.

All actors were social outcasts, the great majority were slaves with no rights as citizens. Rome, unlike Greece, permitted women to act; they were recruited from the slave-class and were legally recognized only as prostitutes, not allowed to engage in any other trade or to marry a patrician. Performers were whipped if they forgot their lines. Those that escaped death-by-performance grew to be greatly loved by the people; some, like Cytheria, by the nobility—Marc Antony had this favourite, a dancer, paraded to all Italy in a chariot drawn by leopards. It is to be doubted whether Nero greatly loved any of his many mistresses but one of them, an actress, certainly seems to have loved him. Following her conversion to Christianity by St Paul, Acte was exiled; but when Nero was on his death-bed she alone of all his followers found a way to his side. Many actresses ran their own companies and wrote plays for them and some rose to great prominence and wealth—Dionysia is recorded to have received the equivalent of £20,000 for a single performance.

One actor, Roscius, amassed such wealth and fame that he was 'freed', honoured by the State and given a welcome by such as Cicero in intellectual society. Students were sent to him for instruction, he served as a model for succeeding generations of actors and his name has become a symbol for praise in his art. He is said to have earned something like half a million pounds a year. Roscius flourished in the first century B.C.; not until over five hundred years later were actors as a class given any citizen rights. It took an actress to do it—and an Emperor. Justinian the Law-giver was infatuated with Theodora, daughter of a Cypriot bear-keeper in the Imperial Circus at Constantinople, actress and courtesan from early years, centre of a thousand scandals, and famed for her mimicry and obscene dancing. He repealed the law in order to marry her. When she became Empress, this astonishing woman, beautiful, witty and impetuous, proved not only a faithful wife but revealed herself as a wise counsellor with great powers of statesmanship, now supporting, now leading 'the first of the Roman emperors to show himself by word and deed the absolute master of the Romans'. She was tolerant, leading the Empire away from religious persecution; she was courageous, rallying the Emperor and his advisers when they thought to take flight from the rioters who took Constantinople; she was pious and built the first home for fallen women in Europe. For twenty-one years an ex-slave shared the throne of a great Emperor as an equal.

Many Christians had died in the theatres of Rome. When the Christian Fathers came to power, the clergy and all devout persons were forbidden to attend the theatres. No player could either become a Christian, or even marry a Christian, unless he quitted the stage. In the sixth century the theatres were finally closed.

In Greece, long ago, religion and the stage had shared in amity the pleasure of illuminating the spirit of man; and the actor was honoured by all. The Roman theatre served

Street-actors, 1568

Two Commedia dell'Arte actors, a trestle-table stage, and an audience of five. This is an (enlarged) detail from *L'Arboro della Pazzia*, 1568. (*Copyright Agne Beijar, Theatre Museum, Drottingholm*)

Market-place theatre, ca. 1672

A Commedia dell'Arte troupe in action in their portable open-air theatre—an enlarged detail from the Jacques Callot series of engravings of Commedia characters, Balli di Sfessania, 1622. (*Copyright Ducharte, Paris*)

Evolution of Mr Punch

Over 2,000 years separate these two illustrations. The present-day Mr Punch of countless Punch and Judy shows shares his profile and other marked similarities with his oldest known antecedent, a terra-cotta statuette now in the Louvre, Paris.

This figure (1) represents one of the actors of the Atellanae, a form of comedy popular in Rome as early as the third century B.C. (*Copyright* (1) *The Louvre, Paris, credited to Giraudon, and* (2) *Mirrorpic*)

Left
Pulcinella 1670

Right
Pulcinella 1680/90

The Italian players had gained great favour in France by the time of Molière, who is portrayed in the same painting that this detail of the actor playing Pulcinella is taken from. It was painted by an unknown artist in 1670 and is now in the collection of the Comédie-Française. (*Copyright Comédie-Française*)

An engraving by the Dutch artist de Geijn (note the hump). (*Copyright Art et Industrie, Paris*)

Left
Pulcinella, eighteenth century

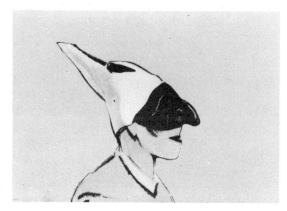

Right
Pulcinella, nineteenth century

This drawing by G. D. Tiepolo (1727–1804) is in the Museo Sartorio, Trieste. Tiepolo's magnificent series of drawings, *La Vita di Pulcinella*, are amongst the very best in which this decorative character has been commemorated. (*Copyright Museo Sartorio, Trieste*)

The actor Antonio Petito was sketched in Naples in 1856 by Jules de Goncourt. Pulcinella was looking very much the same less than ten years ago when I saw him delighting crowds of children in a back-street Naples theatre. Though I didn't understand the language, I found him very funny. (*Copyright Evans Brothers*)

nationalism, not religion; and the actor was debased to a performing beast. The Christian civilization that came to Rome tore down the theatres, banned organized entertainment and drove the actors out of the cities. The Church and the Stage began the long struggle to free themselves from the bonds of love and hate that tie them together. Democracy and one of its most potent voices went underground for centuries.

Footnote to Rome Organized civic theatre had gone, the dramatist and his plays had gone. The actor had taken to the roads, alone or in small troupes. The lone actor was to evolve into the court jester, the ballad-monger and the wandering minstrel. The small troupes who now wandered the countryside found a welcome in the Italian villages where they improvised playlets featuring local peasant characters and dialect. When the actors moved to a new district, the same plots were used incorporating the new characters and dialect. Gradually there evolved a repertoire of 'stock' plots and characters. The peasants and simple townfolk of their audiences were flattered to see themselves as the heroes. The acrobat in the company played the servant, agile of body but slow-witted. He did 'turns' with another servant, quick-brained and sly but physically lazy. There were not many in the simple audience who couldn't enjoy identifying themselves with these two as they tricked doltish peasants and country simpletons. But the real pleasure came from watching all who opposed and 'patronized' them made to look foolish. Many dupes were needed in the list of characters. The old actor in the company played a Rich Man, miserly and vain—or a Professor, long-winded and pedantic, a Doctor (of letters). The middle-aged tragedian found work as the braggart Captain, swaggering and swearing, hiding his coward's heart in ridiculous bombast. The unpractised youngsters in the company played the young Lovers, where looks would tell more than ability. And the singers and dancers filled out the intervals. Rich men and pedants, captains and simpletons, all were duped and tricked, cuffed and kicked. No wonder the actors were popular.

Down the centuries these simple stock characters evolve into the glorious characters of the *Commedia dell'Arte* in its prime. They are still with us—though in somewhat strange mutations. Plain Mr Punch of the English Punch and Judy show is a direct descendant, via France's quick-witted Polichinelle, from Italy's Pulcinella, the Doltish Peasant. Plaintive Pierrot who lends his costume to countless seaside Pierrot troupes wore very much the same costume when he mimicked the simpleton of the Italian villages as Pedrolino. When we talk of a schoolboy's first long pants (or pantaloons) we are recalling Pantalone, the rich old miser who later became Shakespeare's 'lean and slippered' Pantaloon. Harlequin is still with us, his name unchanged though his original costume of tattered patches is now a severely formal uniform of diamond lozenges. The family tree is a large one, its branches everywhere. When the clowns left Italy, they found their way into every court of Europe. They found their way into the plays of Shakespeare and Molière and Goldoni, into circuses as clowns, into pantomimes as Harlequinades. Later they even found their way into films where the immortal Chaplin and Buster Keaton are at least first cousins and Danny Kaye no very distant relation. They first found their way to England in 1673 and they have remained (albeit sadly adulterated) ever since in theatres and circuses, fairgrounds and Punch and Judy shows.

CHAPTER TWO

The Theatre in Early Britain

Two third century Roman theatres have been excavated in Britain—at Caerleon and Verulamium (St Albans). For the six hundred years that follow the departure of the Romans *c*. 400, we have virtually no records of any theatrical activity in this country. The Lombards invaded Rome *c*. 568 and the Roman actor took to the road. He became a wandering minstrel.

The Minstrels Wherever there is a birth, a baptism, a wedding or a time for villagers to rejoice, a minstrel will arrive to entertain with songs and tales. (The priests are instructed to leave before his performance begins.) His fame spreads from country village to nobleman's court, from the nobility of one country to the kings of others. He brings not only songs and tales but news from all over Europe. As the centuries pass, the minstrels grow in number and fame. Rahere, jester to the royal court of Henry I, made a sufficient fortune to found the priory of St Bartholomew at Smithfield, leaving his profession to become its first prior and later, in 1111, prebendary of St Paul's. In 1290, when Margaret of England married John of Brabant, 426 minstrels were present. Schools of minstrelsy were founded in France, guilds of minstrels were formed there in 1321. In 1469 the English guilds were formed. The early fifteenth century finds them (known as 'waits') wearing town livery and in the service of the city corporations of London and the larger provincial centres. There seems little doubt that the minstrel and other solo performers, jesters, singing ballad-mongers, acrobats and their like were the staple fare of entertainment for the six hundred years or so that separate the departure of the Romans from our first records of English drama.

Miracle Plays Though the story of world theatre is some three thousand years old, the   15

The Roman theatre of Verulamium (St Albans)

The only completely exposed ruins of a Roman theatre known in England. First, constructed c. A.D. 140, the final rebuilding seems to have taken place c. A.D. 300. Evidence from refuse and broken pottery etc. indicated that by the latter half of the fourth century A.D., the theatre had become a rubbish dump, though it is not wholly clear why literally thousands of Roman coins were also discovered on the site. The ground plan bears some resemblance to the earlier form of Greek theatres. (*Copyright Aerofilms Ltd*)

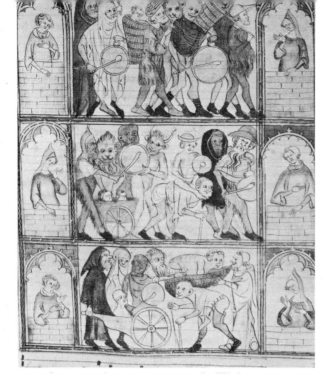

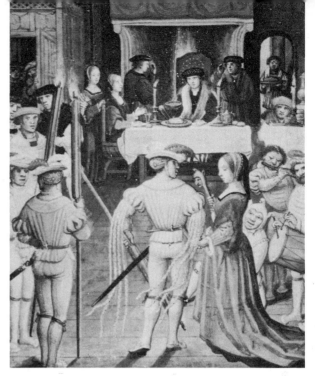

Fourteenth century minstrels

Animal disguises now serve a purely secular purpose as illustrated in these panels of early fourteenth century minstrels from a manuscript, *Le Roman de Fauvel*, by de Bus, now in the Bibliothèque Nationale. (*Copyright Bibliothèque Nationale*)

Fifteenth–sixteenth century minstrels

A more courtly kind of minstrel than that shown in the preceding illustration is shown in this Flanders manuscript, *c*. 1500, now in the British Museum. (*Copyright British Museum*)

recorded history of the English drama only goes back some eight hundred years. Between 1100 and 1200, there are several references in old documents to performances of what we call Miracle Plays. How they evolved can only be conjectured. Perhaps the starting-point is with that charming feature of Christmas, familiar to this day, the little Nativity group of dressed dolls clustering round the crib. At some point, this group of dolls was replaced by a 'still-life' group in which the Holy Family were represented by dressed-up priests. This in turn elaborated into a group who spoke a short Nativity playlet. In time the plays got longer; they were given more often: and soon they revealed a wider range of subjects, chosen from the Bible and the lives of the saints.

The Miracle Plays were simple tales, lavishly adorned with spectacle, written and acted by priests in churches for an audience of simple folk, largely illiterate, whom the Church hoped to convert. When there was not room enough in the churches for all the people who wanted to see them, the performances were moved out-of-doors—first adjoining the church and later in the largest available open space in the town centre, usually the market-place. Slowly, over the years, the performances changed character, crude knock-about scenes of everyday life encroaching on the religious stories. Soon the tradesmen took over the acting from the priests and it was not long before they were joined by strolling professionals, jugglers, acrobats and their like.

Guilds of tradesmen were formed to organize the performances, each electing a 'pageant master'. A yearly subscription was levied from all their members so that no expense might be spared in the elaborate and painstaking preparation of the plays. In

17

Acting in church

The Church was used as a theatre, with priests as actors, in early England, *c.* 1100 A.D. It was the first stage in the evolution of our written drama. The Hans Holbein engraving of a performance in a church shows that this custom continued for many years and was very much more a dramatic performance than a religious ritual

time different Guilds came to specialize in different plays. At York the Shipwrights appropriately presented Noah's Ark. Noah, his family and 'divers animals' fell to the lot of the Fishmongers and Mariners. The Vintners (wine-makers) took care of the Marriage celebrations at Cana, the Chandlers looked after the Star in the East and the offerings of the Three Kings came from the Goldsmiths.

The stages on which the plays were performed were movable—over-sized and rather solid carts, the sort of trucks used in today's Lord Mayor's processions. These structures were of two storeys, sometimes even three. The upper storey was the stage proper and this was open on three sides to give the audience all round it a better view. The lower storey was closed in with curtains. Here the actors made their changes—and from here Devils popped their heads up through trap-doors. These carts needed to be very solid structures and one is not surprised to find that they were not destroyed at the end of each year's performance but put into storage (5*s.* a year). Later on, a succession of carts was used; the audience stayed in their places whilst successive scenes and incidents moved past them, each with their own cart. At Wakefield as many as thirty carts were used.

A stage open on three sides does not allow for very great scenic opportunities, but it would be wrong to suppose that there were none. We know that an imitation Ark was erected for the flood scenes in Noah. Changes of locality were indicated by altering the tapestry that hung at the back of the stage—'half a yard of Red Sea' for example. Stage effects included a 'Barrell for the Earthquake', 'Starch to make the Storm' and it is recorded that a man was paid for 'Setting the World on Fire'. Great care was taken with

18

Acting on pageant-wagons in the streets

Though this engraving is a conjectural reconstruction made at a much later date (1825) by David Jee to illustrate Sharp's *Dissertation on the Pageants or Dramatic Mysteries Anciently performed at Coventry*, it gives a good idea of what the performances of the Miracle plays must have been like in the Middle Ages. Wagon followed wagon as each successive scene was enacted in the Coventry Miracle play (this scene pictures Jesus before Pilate). (*Copyright Huntington Library, California*)

Pageant-wagons in the streets

This detail from the paintings by Denis van Alsloot of *Isabella's Triumph* shows the streets of Brussels in 1615. It indicates what rich elaboration the pageants permitted. The full paintings reveal numerous such wagons. Biblical scenes share the celebration in welcome companionship with mythological scenes—that of the Annunciation, for example, is hotly pursued by the wagon containing Diana and her nymphs. The paintings are in the Victoria and Albert Museum. (*Copyright Victoria and Albert Museum*)

the costumes. God was dressed in white and his face was of gold. The Devil had clothes of rough, hairy stuff, horns, a tail and a red beard.

In the earliest days of the Miracle Plays, the audiences happily accepted many conventions that would seem strange to us. The story they watched had to be acted out in front of a bench on which were sitting those actors who had either finished or not yet started their parts. This convention was born of necessity for there was no way that the actors could leave the stage-cart. Nor could the prompter be hidden; he remained in sight, armed with a book and a wand, pointing with the latter to each character in turn as they were due to speak. In some instances, the prompter stood just behind the actors giving them their speeches line by line so that they wouldn't have to commit them to memory. Some gentlemanly joker in Cornwall in 1602 once took the place of one of the actors. When the prompter whispered to him what he was to say, he said something else. 'Oh, you marre the play' whispered the prompter. This, too, was repeated. The prompter lost his temper and let fly with a whispered torrent of oaths. These, too, were repeated. The performance broke up in disorder, the audience were dismissed and the prompter was in a 'madde rage'. The chronicler records that there was 'a great deale more sport and laughter' than twenty such performances normally afforded.

The priests who acted in the early Miracle Plays were paid for performing. As late as 1511 'a brotherhood priest' received 2s. 8d. for prompting a play about St George. The later guild-players were not only paid quite handsomely but given their food and drink during rehearsals. The sums paid to those impersonating various important characters are not without their humour. The Devil and Judas each got 1s. 6d., God a little more (2s.) and Herod as much as 3s. 4d. (Herod called for great reserves of energy in that he spent most of his time in a prolonged state of rage.) At a time when a rib of beef and a goose cost sixpence and a gallon of ale twopence, an author commissioned to write *The Destruction of Jerusalem* for £13 6s. 8d. seems very well paid.

Great care was taken in the presentation of the plays. The guild-players were subject to very heavy discipline from the civic authorities. They were fined forty shillings if they failed to bring forth their pageant-carts 'at the places that is assigned therefor and nowhere else'—this moreover at between four and five o'clock in the chill before sunrise. Further, the Guild was fined one hundred shillings if their players were not 'good players, well arrayed and openly speaking'.

Morality Plays and Interludes In the fifteenth century a new kind of play came into being. The most famous of these is *Everyman*. The story represents Everyman's successive experiences with characters typifying the various Virtues and Vices. In this and other Morality Plays, characters like Wisdom, Sobriety and Obedience triumph over Pride, Avarice and Gluttony. A succession of less austere characters like Dinner, Supper, Banquet, Colic, Dropsy, Pill and Bad Luck seem to indicate livelier performances. But, for the most part, they are too severely stylized to kindle overmuch warmth. Soon there emerged a shortened form, known as Moral Interludes. As the actors moved out from the shadow of the Church, these in turn became plain (secular) Interludes.

The later Miracle pageant plays had called for hundreds of actors and spectacular

The unhidden prompter, a priest dominates and conducts a grisly performance of *The Martyrdom of St Apollonia.* One cannot but feel that the trusting actress deserved canonisation as well. Hell seems to be on the right and Heaven on the left, and the intervening mansions no doubt illustrate the intermediate state we call life. This is a fifteenth century miniature by Jean Fouquet. (*Copyright Musée Condé, Chantilly, France*)

presentation with increasingly elaborate settings. They were expensive to produce and impossible to move around. The 'List of Characters' at the head of extant copies of Interludes often stresses that certain parts could be doubled. They could be acted by half-a-dozen people, required little or no scenery, were cheap to produce, and could be easily travelled. They were, in fact, made to order for the small groups of strolling players who were now beginning to frequent the country.

Six players and a cart could travel with quite an extensive repertoire of Interludes, playing on village greens or in country inn-yards. From these, however, they were quite often 'moved on' by the less tolerant local authorities. Their next port of call would almost certainly be the great house of a local noble. Here, in the banqueting hall, they would be sure of a welcome—if they could match their host's tastes. Most, no doubt, could be matched 'from stock' whether edifying moralities for the pious or after-supper cabaret for the rollickers. There was, however, a growing minority of nobles who were developing more esoteric tastes. The titles of such Interludes as *The Nature of the Four Elements* and *The Marriage of Wit and Science* indicate that the players were now having to stretch their minds. The afternoon's simple mummery on the village green was quickly followed by the evening's erudite Interlude in the banqueting hall. (Another Interlude, *Gentleness and Nobility*, in which a knight and a ploughman discuss 'what makes a gentleman' shrewdly caters for both markets.)

The Medieval Theatre—A Summary The Miracle Plays were the staple fare of entertainment for some four hundred years, the last hundred of which they shared with Morali-

Devil's Costume in the Middle Ages

The illustration on the right, taken from Barclay's
Ship of Fools, shows how the Middle Ages
pictured the devil.

It is remarkably similar to an actual costume
(above)—traditional in the Tyrol—which was
still in existence in a private collection until
destroyed by fire during 1914–1918 war.
Note also the traditional long ears of the fool.
*(Copyright Max Hermann, Forschungen,
Germany; and Allardyce Nicoll)*

ties and Interludes. They began by being the sort of play that the priests wanted. They became the sort of play that the people wanted. With the closing of the Middle Ages, the ground is laid for the sort of plays that educated authors will want and the arrival of the first English tragedies and comedies.

The first players were priests. They were superseded by the guild-players, part-time semi-professionals giving occasional paid performances at the yearly celebrations. They in turn were superseded by the full-time professionals. The great majority of these were 'common players', strollers who could give no performance without a licence from the local Justice of the Peace on danger of prosecution as 'rogues and vagabonds'. Others, more fortunate, found patronage under the great noblemen. Most fortunate of all were those who became a permanent part of the household staff of the first King to become a patron of the players—Richard III.

Prelude to Gloriana It is impossible to comprehend how the settled glories of Shakespeare and the Elizabethan theatre could have evolved from the relatively crude and naïve plays of the troubled Middle Ages, without some knowledge of what had been happening in the world outside the theatre. Some seventy years separate the death of Richard III from the crowning of Elizabeth, and they see the coming of the Renaissance.

Ten years before Richard died, the printing press had come to an England in which the Roman clergy held a virtual monopoly of education and culture. Men began to take their thoughts from the new books and learned to question the long tyranny of an alien Church. Seventeen years after the coming of the printing press—in the very year that Columbus set sail for the new world—a Spaniard, one of the rich Borgias, had left for Rome, having bribed the Church to make him Pope. It became apparent that the Pope was appointed not by God but by priests as venal as their counterparts in England; and Englishmen began to think about seeking some way to God that would not involve paying tribute to Rome.

Many were now asking that love of one's country should offer something more than incessant war-service; education something more than Rome was teaching; and religion something more than the support of idle monks who sold masses and split the profits with Rome. At this point English thinking was invaded by (among others) a gentle Dutch scholar, who for thirteen years held a chair of divinity at Cambridge and gave a voice and direction to the new thought. Erasmus spoke not with the hectoring voice of the fanatic reformer, but in disarming tones of moderation and good humour. He was both a man of God and an enlightened radical humanist. His books asked men to reject the outward trappings of a Church increasingly given to superstition and to go back to the simple text of the Scriptures, which were to be translated into every language so that the farmer might 'say them to himself as he follows the plough' and the weaver 'hum them to the tune of his shuttle'. Wherever ideas had wandered from their past purity to present abuses, he called men back. Further, he called men forward out of their narrow nationalisms to a vision of a united Europe. Book after book tumbled from the busy printing presses and Erasmus found himself the author of the first secular 'best-sellers' with many eager readers. Men began to flex their minds.

Erasmus—a detail from an engraving by Albrecht Durer, 1526. (*Copyright British Museum*)

This Age of Protest brought about by Erasmus and his fellow reformers created a climate of thought in which it became possible for Henry VIII to risk the great gamble of separation from Rome and, later, the dissolution of the monasteries. The point was not far off when England would emerge as an independent nation, denying the heavy tribute it had long paid abroad; and when its sovereign would be able to command a united front at least to any threat of foreign invasion. For the moment it was a country divided within itself and all men found that they must take sides in the bitter conflict that Henry's action had provoked—even the actors.

When the players and their public had moved out from under the shadow of the Church, the actors had been dubbed 'anti-papist' and now the majority found that their sympathies lay that way, with the new Humanists and with their Sovereign. Yet the Papist voice was still a strong one and many actors found themselves supporting it. Both groups were much harried by the State as successive monarchs sought to establish their precarious hold on a divided people. In unsettled times, authority always has to look with a wary eye on any large gatherings of people and few were larger than those that assembled for the players. Proclamation followed proclamation, seeking to limit the players' rights and castigating them as 'disseminators of sedition and heresies'.

The players' stories had greatly changed from the old dusty tales of saints and gods. With *The Famous Victories of Henry V* and others of the many Chronicle plays that were now finding favour, it was the real figures of recent history that peopled the plays. The playwrights, long ago in the Miracle Plays, had learnt to record the precise tones of everyday speech, the minute details of human behaviour. The stage was learning to hold up the mirror to real people who spoke with contemporary voices. Above all, it reflected the new wonder in words. 'The word' had long lain slumbering; now, as men's minds stretched and grew, it leapt into life. And the whole liberated community, lettered and unlettered alike, set sail to discover and explore the great New Worlds of thought.

CHAPTER THREE

The Elizabethan Theatre

Nothing, it seems, will stop us thinking of Shakespeare as an Elizabethan. The Queen came to the throne six years before he was born; his first plays were not performed until three-quarters of her forty-five year reign was over; she was dead before *Hamlet* was performed; this, all the other major tragedies and more than half his total output came in James's reign. It is a matter of mood not of dates—Shakespeare swims with the tide of Elizabeth, against that of James.

What plays were the mileposts on the road to Shakespeare? The first English comedy appeared early in the decade before Elizabeth came to the throne. Compared with Shakespeare's comedies, it seems a child among men; compared with what went before it is a giant among pigmies. Scholarly minds, both at court and in the schools, were at this time greatly influenced by Italy and it is to that influence that *Ralph Roister Doister* owes what must have seemed revolutionarily novel at the time—the shaping of its plot. The domestic humours of its middle-class characters are wholly English. It was written by Nicholas Udall, headmaster of Eton and Westminster. The second comedy, *Gammer Gurton's Needle*, is also a 'school' play and was performed at Cambridge University. Though its unknown author would have needed the most up to date scholarship to construct his play as he did, he was no lofty academic. The play is knock-about farce, its homely villagers are true to life, its dialogue racy—and the lads who played it must have had great fun. We can hear the monstrous thwacking and thumping, see the chasing and missing, the catching and thrashing as they curse each other: 'Come out, hog. Thou arrant witch! Thou bawdy bitch! Thou slut! Thou scald! Thou bald! Thou rotten!' *The Taming of the Shrew* is not all that far off. (Both these 'school' comedies were later taken up by the professional actors. Nearly forty years later we find the *Gammer* in the repertoire of a group of English actors playing

25

Queen Elizabeth as patron of the arts

George Gascoigne solicits the patronage of his Queen. He was both soldier and man of letters, a poet and dramatist. He had served his Queen fighting in the Low Countries; she had expressed her pleasure with his prose tale, *Hemetes the Heremyte*. The illustration appeared as frontispiece to the copy of the work he presented to her and is followed by a dedicatory sonnet in which he asks how best he may serve her. (The Royal Manuscript is in the British Museum, reference MS Royal 18 A xlviii.) (*Copyright British Museum*)

at Frankfurt Fair in Germany. Their leader, Robert Browne, for something like thirty years recruited companies to tour Europe with English plays.)

Four years after she came to the throne, Elizabeth attended a performance given in her honour of what is commonly accepted as the first English tragedy. *Gorbuduc* was written and acted by the gentlemen of the Inner Temple for an audience of lawyers and their friends. It marks the arrival of the five-act form of tragedy and the use for the first time in any play of blank verse; but, though the play is historically important, one suspects that the Queen must have had rather a yawnful time. Certainly the play, written by scholars for private performance to scholars, would have had too austere a dignity for the lively popular theatre. Eight years or so later, the professional players were seen limbering up for the great exercises that lay ahead by performing a play that the academics would have dismissed as having too little dignity. *Cambises* by Thomas Preston is 'neither right tragedy nor right comedy, mingling kings and clowns'; it is, in fact, the first tragi-comedy. The academics might be uneasy about the lack of any classical precedent for mingling in such close proximity a king's tears and a clown's laughter, but the poets and the people were seeking a truth that might only be found in freedom from such alien rules. The play is crude and straggling in form, but bustling and lively in mood; written to be popular, it was played in the public theatre.

The Queen's interest in plays appears to have been no mere duty, forced upon a reluctant sovereign by the formal routine of court etiquette, but a genuinely personal interest as unfailingly delightful to her as our own Queen's interest in horses. Some six to ten plays were given every winter at court and she saw many others when in progress through the country or attending weddings and banquets in London. Throughout the forty-five years of her reign, she protected the players when their enemies in the clergy and the City sought to 'put them down'. Moreover she encouraged her nobles to form new companies to compete with the old. With twenty or so companies in competition, standards fast began to improve.

For the first eighteen years of the reign, most public performances had taken place in the inn-yards, played on a 'fit-up' platform on trestles. In 1576 the first English public theatre was built. Its structure echoed that of the inn-yards but its stage was more permanent, useful for rehearsals and encouraging to mild scenic experiment. Though the theatre cost its builders some £700* to erect, it no doubt proved a sound investment, freeing the players from having to pay rent to inn-landlords and bringing them extra revenue from the sale of food and wine within the theatre. Above all, it gave them the opportunity to be masters in their own house. The Theatre, as the new playhouse was called, stood for some twenty years. The Curtain, built a year later, stood for fifty years.

In the same year that The Theatre was built, the most famous of the Boy Actors, the Children of the Chapel, first appeared in (what amounted to) public performances in the 'private' theatre at Blackfriars. Under the auspices of Church and School, they had a long tradition behind them and were great favourites at Court. (In the ten years preceding this date, of some sixty performances given at Court, thirty-five were given by the boys as against twenty-five by the men. In the following ten years, the balance is reversed, the men

* Ten or eleven times more in our money.

giving about fifty, twice as many as the boys.) They found great favour at Blackfriars. They became quasi-professionals and their plays were no longer 'school' plays but written by major Elizabethan dramatists—Lyly, Middleton, Marston, Dekker and Ben Jonson. The dramatists in no way limited the character of their plays when writing for the Boy Players. There were pretty pastorals and brawling farces enough but also topical satire and this was so savage that, on one occasion, Lyly embroiled the boys deep enough in the controversies of religion and politics for their performances to be suppressed for a time. (We have to be on our guard against thinking of all the boys as angelic little choir-boys, hastily scrubbed, combed and bundled onto the stage to pipe their well-drilled way through the lines. Nat Field was twenty-one at the time he was entrusted by Ben Jonson with a leading part in one of the many plays he wrote for the boys. Many, no doubt, were younger than this. The best were very expert indeed and many later found their way into the adult companies, where they acted the female characters, there being no actresses at this period.)

Seven years later three of the Boy Companies united as the Children of Blackfriars to give Lyly's *Campaspe*. Lyly is so often carelessly equated solely with the sort of flowery overwriting that characterizes much of his most famous work, the novel *Euphues*, that two lines from *Campaspe* may serve to put him into truer focus:

KING ALEXANDER: How happened it that you would not come out of your tub to my palace?
DIOGENES: Because it was as far from my tub to your palace as from your palace to my tub.

One wonders how the Queen reacted to this robust democratic sentiment when she witnessed a command performance.

Four years later, and only some three or four years before Shakespeare began writing, *The Spanish Tragedy* was first seen. Its author, Thomas Kyd, was a man of the theatre—and the play is nothing if not theatrical, a gallimaufry of all the ingredients that have popularized melodrama ever since. Blood and pomp, revenge, splendour and madness tread on each other's heels; and, at curtain-fall, a ghost contentedly catalogues no less than seven murders and two suicides in no more than nine lines of verse. The play has come in for much ridicule but, though its verse at worst plunges from rant to bathos, at its best it is far from despicable:

> The blustering winds, conspiring with my words,
> At my lament have moved the leafless trees,
> Disrobed the meadows of their flowered green,
> Made mountains marsh with springtide of my tears,
> And broken through the brazen gates of hell;

This is something more than 'penny knave's delight'. The play was overwhelmingly popular, even later when it had to compete with plays by Shakespeare; and it provided a magnificent part for Edward Alleyn, the first of the great English actors.

The same year, 1587, saw the coming of a dramatist beside whom Kyd and his predecessors pale into insignificance. With Marlowe's 'mighty line', blank verse and the

Kyd's 'Spanish tragedy'

The illustration is from the title-page of the 1615 edition. We have no way of knowing whether this in any way represents the stage presentation, with Alleyn as Hieronomo. (*Copyright British Museum*)

Marlowe's 'Doctor Faustus'

The illustration is from the title-page of the 1636 edition. Again, as with Kyd's *Spanish Tragedy*, we have no way of knowing whether this represents Alleyn in the part. The hint of Mephistopheles's mask and costume (and his appearance through a trap in the stage) are worth noting. (*Copyright British Museum*)

English drama come of age. It is very much the day of youth. Marlowe, a cobbler's son, is twenty-three when Alleyn at twenty-one launches *Tamburlaine*. (Is Shakespeare, also twenty-three, there? We do not know; it is five years later that he is recorded as an established actor and dramatist. Or twenty-year-old Richard Burbage, who is to inherit Alleyn's mantle as First Player? Again, we don't know, but three years later he is in the company, playing a 'walk-on' messenger. Or the seventeen-year-old Ben Jonson? Again, no record. All that is certain is that all three of them, and many of the others who were to grace the age, clearly experience the liberation that Marlowe and Alleyn together are giving to the stage.) Marlowe's second play on *Tamburlaine* follows when he is twenty-four, *Dr Faustus* at twenty-five, *The Jew of Malta* at twenty-six and *Edward II* at twenty-seven. Now at last the age finds a dramatist who is no mere stepping-stone to Shakespeare but a giant in his own right. Listen to Faustus putting aside God and his Bible and see how Kyd pales beside Marlowe's majesty:

> What doctrine call you this, *Che sera sera*,
> What will be, shall be? Divinity, adieu! . . .
> All things that move between the quiet poles
> Shall be at my command: emperors and kings
> Are but obeyed in their several provinces,
> Nor can they raise the wind or rend the clouds;
> But his dominion that exceeds in this
> Stretcheth as far as doth the mind of man:
> A sound magician is a mighty god. . . .

Listen to Faustus extolling Helen:

> Oh thou art fairer than the evening air
> Clad in the beauty of a thousand stars

and, finally, facing his destiny:

> Now hast thou but one bare hour to live,
> And then thou must be damned perpetually;
> Stand still you ever-moving spheres of heaven,
> That time may cease, and midnight never come.
> Fair nature's eye, rise, rise again and make
> Perpetual day, or let this hour be but
> A year, a month, a week, a natural day,
> That Faustus may repent and save his soul.
> *O lente, lente currite noctis equi:*
> The stars move still, time runs, the clock will strike,
> The devil will come, and Faustus must be damn'd.
> O I'll leap up to my God: who pulls me down?
> See, see where Christ's blood streams in the firmament.
> One drop would save my soul, half a drop, ah my Christ. . . .

30

Listen to Tamburlaine and hear, surely, Marlowe's own voice:

> If all the pens that ever poets held
> Had fed the feeling of their master's thoughts,
> And every sweetness that inspired their hearts,
> Their minds and muses on admired themes;
> If all the heavenly quintessence they still
> From their immortal flowers of poesy,
> Wherein, as in a mirror, we perceive
> The highest reaches of a human wit;
> If these had made one poem's period
> And all combined in beauty's worthiness,
> Yet should there hover in their restless heads
> One thought, one grace, one wonder, at the least,
> Which into words no virtue can digest. . . .

At twenty-nine, Marlowe was dead, killed brawling over the bill for a day's drinking. 'Cut is the branch that might have grown full straight.' What might he not have done had he lived? What might not have been done, had he not lived? It is Marlowe's music and mastery that is ringing in Shakespeare's ears when he takes up his pen to write.

Nothing so becomes Edward Alleyn as his patronage of Marlowe, with whom he raised the arts of the stage to heights hitherto unknown. Alleyn 'was bred a stage-player' and rose in the ranks with astonishing rapidity. He was only twenty-one when he appeared in *The Spanish Tragedy* and in *Tamburlaine*, in which he began the association with Marlowe that was to continue by his appearance at twenty-two in *The Second Part of Tamburlaine*, at twenty-three in *Dr Faustus* and at twenty-four in *The Jew of Malta*. At twenty-six he married his manager Henslowe's daughter and at thirty-one was rich enough to retire. Thereafter he added greatly to his wealth by building new theatres in association with Henslowe. In 1600 the Fortune was built at a cost of £440* for the freehold and £520* for the building. It was to appear at this theatre that (pressed by the Queen) he returned from retirement when thirty-four until he finally gave up acting at thirty-seven. At forty-eight he founded Dulwich College which he built at a cost of £10,000* and continued to administrate at a cost of £1,700* a year. Shrewd in his investments, pious in their disposal, he showed an equal dignity in his private affairs and public appearances. A French visitor recorded 'a pleasing voice, a good figure, and a fine presence' and Ben Jonson said that he 'outstript . . . all who went before . . . others spake but only thou dost act'.

Richard Burbage, Alleyn's rival and successor, is thought to have begun his acting career when he was seventeen. When he was twenty-three he is mentioned as 'scornfully and disdainfully playing with his deponent's nose' in a brawl, in which, armed with a broom, he was fending off claims on his father's theatre, where he is listed as walking on in Alleyn's company. At twenty-five he and Shakespeare were at the head of a breakaway company and two years later they were rising to the prominence they achieved at the Globe, built when Burbage was thirty-two. The ten years that followed saw Burbage as the original

* Ten or eleven times more in our money.

The two great Elizabethan actors—Alleyn and Burbage

From contemporary paintings, both in Dulwich College Collection. (*Copyright Dulwich College*)

Hamlet, Othello, Lear and Richard III. (Apropos the latter, there is an engaging entry in John Manningham's diary (1602) recalling, 'Upon a time when Burbage played Rich. 3 there was a citizen grew so far in liking with him, that before she went from the play she appointed him to come that night unto her by the name of Richard the Third. Shakespeare, overhearing their conclusion, went before, was entertained, and at his game ere Burbage came. Then, message being brought that "Richard the Third" was at the door, Shakespeare caused return to be made that William the Conqueror was before Richard the Third. Shakespeare's name, William.') Burbage also played leading parts in Ben Jonson's *Volpone* and *The Alchemist*, in Webster's *Duchess of Malfi* and took over Alleyn's old part in *The Spanish Tragedy*. Though his brother, Cuthbert, later spoke of the '35 year's pains, cost and labour' in which Burbage struggled to provide for his family, contemporary gossip says that he left better than £300* a year in land. As an actor, he stood supreme, as Ben Johnson testified in *Bartholomew Fair* where he says: 'Where is your Burbage now . . . your best actor?' When he died (1619) at the age of fifty-two, his foolish-fond audience mourned his death as much as they had that of their Queen.

'On the 21st September' 1599, one Thomas Platter, a visitor from Basle, 'saw the tragedy of the first Emperor Julius with at least fifteen characters very well acted.' This was

32   * Ten or eleven times more in our money.

Shakespeare's *Julius Caesar* and the theatre was the Globe, built on Bankside by Richard Burbage and his brother on land leased for thirty-one years and held jointly 'in two equal moieties' by them and five actors of the Chamberlain's company, of whom Shakespeare was one. This was now the dominant company, seen at Court thirty-two times during Elizabeth's reign as against twenty visits by its nearest rival, the Admiral's men, and thirteen by all others. With Burbage acting and Shakespeare writing, the Globe became the centre of theatrical activity for the ten years that followed its opening.

Elizabethan Theatre—A General Picture You are up from the country. You've come to Queen Elizabeth's London to stay for a few days with relations at their house in the suburbs. It stands, like a farmer's cottage, looking out over the fields in what is now called Leicester Square. Climb to the top of the tallest tree in the back meadow and look round you. To the north, the gentle countryside stretches away to the distant hills of Hampstead. To the west, you see the magnificent palace of Whitehall; Westminster beyond: and further, as the Thames winds westward, the scattered palaces and mansions of the great nobles that dot the countryside. Now turn to the east. Here the smoke rises from the myriad chimneys of London proper—the City. In the shadow of the Tower, house huddles upon house 'five or six roofs high' in the bustling heart of this 'excellent and mighty city of business', where 'one can scarcely pass along the streets, on account of the throng'. Paul's Walk 'is a heap of stones and men, with a vast confusion of languages. . . . The noise . . . mixed of walking, tongues and feet . . . is a kind of still roar or loud whisper . . . no business whatsoever but is here stirring and afoot. . . . All inventions are emptied here, and not few pockets'. In Cheapside and 'every street, carts and coaches make such a thundering as if the world ran upon wheels: at every corner, men, women and children meet in such shoals . . . here are porters, sweating under burdens, there merchant's men bearing bags of money'. London Bridge, 'to be numbered among the miracles of the world', straddles the busy Thames, 'the glory and wealth of the city, the highway to the sea, the bringer in of wealth and strangers'. Turn a little to the south and there, over the river on Bankside, the great wooden O's of the stately Playhouses tower over the surrounding dwellings.

A play is to be given this afternoon and, as you walk to Westminster, the talk is all of playhouse matters. Of how the clergy rail against the 'gorgeous' and 'sumptuous' playhouse as a 'Chapel of Satan' and 'a shew-place of all beastly and filthy matters' where 'if you will learn to care neither for Heaven nor Hell, and to commit all kinds of sin and mischief, you need go to no other school'. Yet 'Will not a filthy play, with the blast of a trumpet, sooner call thither a thousand, than an hour's tolling of a bell bring to the sermon a hundred?' But 'mark the flocking and running to theatres and curtains, daily and hourly, night and day, time and tide, to see plays and interludes'. You talk, too, of how the Lord Mayor and Aldermen (spurred thereto no doubt by priests and city usurers alike) wrote to the Privy Council that 'stage-plays were the very places of their rendezvous' for idle apprentices and 'masterless men to come together', for 'evil-disposed and ungodly people . . . to assemble themselves . . . for their lewd and ungodly practices' and pleaded for 'the present stay and final suppressing of the said stage-plays'.

You recall how Nashe, one of the player's writers, had forthrightly replied: 'Whereas

Swan   *Bear-Garden*   Glo

Shakespeare's London

the afternoon, being the idlest time of the day, wherein men that are their own masters . . . do wholly bestow themselves upon pleasure . . . either into gaming, following of harlots, drinking, or seeing a play: is it not then better (since of four extremes all the world cannot keep them but they will choose one) that they should betake them to the least, which is plays? Nay, what if I prove plays to be no extreme, but a rare exercise of virtue? First, for the subject of them (for the most part) it is borrowed out of our English chronicles, wherein our forefather's valiant acts (that have lain long buried in rusty brass and worm-eaten books) are revived. . . . There is no immortality can be given a man on earth like unto plays. . . . What talk I to them of immortality, that are only the underminers of honour, and do envy any man that is not sprung up by base brokery like themselves? . . . If you tell them what a glorious thing it is to have Henry V represented on the stage. . . . "Aye but" (will they say) "what do we get by it?" . . . As for the hindrance of trades and traders of the city by them, that is an article foisted in by the vintners, alewives and victuallers, who surmise, if there were no plays, they should have all the company that resort to them lie boozing and beer-bathing in their houses every afternoon.' You talk of the rival merits of the twenty-odd companies of players that compete for public favour, five or six of which are now in London. Of how often these companies have toured the country places. (The young Shakespeare, between his tenth and twenty-fourth years, could have witnessed no less that twenty-three visits from the players even in so small a market town as Stratford.) You talk of that same Shakespeare, who came from a provincial grammar school to eclipse the university M.A. playwrights. You talk of the five theatres that have been built in London since 1576 when the great actor Burbage's father built the first of them all. You talk of the wit of the younger Burbages who—when that Theatre in Shoreditch was forced to close by the Privy Council

A section from Visscher's *View of London*, 1616; the best of the earliest illustrations to include the playhouses. They are, from left to right, the Swan, the Bear-Garden and the Globe, with the grisly heads on Traitor's Gate at the extreme right. (*Copyright Guildhall Library*)

and complicated lawsuits were threatening to rob the brothers of their investment—took the theatre to pieces, stick by stick, and rebuilt it on Bankside as the Globe. You talk of Tarleton, the comedian, the Queen's own favourite in the company that the Master of Revels recruited when he was ordered to travel the country to 'choose out a company of players for Her Majesty'. And of Alleyn who, only two years ago, had made a sufficient fortune by the theatre and wise investment to retire at the early age of thirty-one. Of how rich the actors must be when even 'the very hirelings of some of our players . . . jet it under gentleman's noses in suits of silk'.

By now your walk has brought you to the river at Westminster where a great throng of watermen 'keep such a bawling' as they beckon for playhouse passengers. Soon your boatman has jostled his way out into the main stream of traffic that goes jigging up the broad highway of the Thames. (There are some thirty to forty thousand watermen among London's two hundred thousand people.) You are one of a myriad of small craft whose sculls thresh the water as you go bobbing and bouncing through the wash of the great trade-bound sailing ships. The clock strikes twelve as you clamber up the steps at Bankside. You hurry to the tavern; it is high noon and time to dine for the plays begin at two.

Done with the tavern, there is time to walk round a district 'as dirty as Smithfield and as stinking every whit'. Through the Stews where the brothels cluster by the Clink (prison). Past the Bear-gardens, towards which a cart is lumbering with its load of butcher's garbage for the bears and bulls, caged nearby till they meet in the Ring where 'fastened behind' they will be 'worried by those great English dogs and mastiffs, but not without great risk to the dogs from the teeth of the one and the horns of the other'; past the pond

*The
Elizabethan
Theatre*

35

where have been thrown the snapping dogs that died in yesterday's baiting. ('Here are cruel beasts in it, and as basely used; here are foul beasts come to it, and as bad or worse keep it . . . fitter for a wilderness than a city.') Out past the stinking sewers to the fresher air of the little market gardens that border on the more formal park of Paris Gardens. Back round by the riverside to see the Royal Barge 'kept upon dry ground' so that its two 'splendid cabins, beautifully ornamented with glass windows, painting and gilding' may be 'sheltered from the weather'. Finally, passing the two smaller theatres, the Rose and the Swan, you come in sight of the flag that flutters from the roof of the Globe, proclaiming that there is to be a play this afternoon. 'Heaving, and shoving, itching and shouldering' you are swept along in the great stream of eager humanity, 'the swaggering roarer, the cunning cheater, the rotten bawd, the swearing drunkard and the bloody butcher' among others less noxious.

'Thus every day at two o'clock . . . two and sometimes three comedies are performed, at separate places, wherewith folk make merry together.' You pay your penny* at the outer door and pass into the yard that surrounds three sides of the raised platform of the stage. Here those that can afford no more will stand throughout the 'two-hours' traffic' of the play. 'There are, however, separate galleries and there one stands more comfortably and moreover can sit, but one pays more for it.' You pay a further penny* and go through a further door to one of the galleries. If you wish 'to sit on a cushion in the most comfortable place of all where' you not only see 'everything well, but can also be seen', then you give 'yet another English penny* at another door'. (If today were the first performance of a new play, you would have had to pay double at each door.) The pennies go into a locked box, some of which will go to the landlords by way of rent, the rest to the actors. Both are pitifully dependent on the money-takers who have developed an occupational habit 'to scratch their heads where they itch not' and drop coins 'in at the collars'. (Dekker dedicating one of his plays to the actors, wryly wishes them 'a full audience and one honest door-keeper'.)

If it rains, you will be dry under the thatched roof that shelters the three 'horseshoe' galleries that advance their arms to the stage within the circular playhouse. The players, too, can find partial shelter under the 'shadow or cover' that tops the pillars that rise from the stage floor. But the 'standing' yard that surrounds three sides of the stage is open to the skies so that the stage may have light. Now when the yard, 'the belly of the stage', is but half full let us look at the motley crowd that presses in. Here are 'Knights . . . Templars . . . Fleet-street gentlemen . . . and sweet courtiers' but 'your gallant, your courtier and your captain' are 'the soundest pay-masters'. Nevertheless the 'groundling and gallery-commoner . . . the rude, rascal rabble . . . the tag-rag people' come hither for their 'penny knave's delight', have 'the same liberty' as the courtiers, be they 'waiting-women or gentleman ushers . . . country serving men . . . farmer's son . . . carman . . . tinkers or stinkards'. Here, too, come those with free passes. Neither poets, playwrights nor pamphleteers (nor even their pages) are called on to pay.

'It is the fashion of youths to go first into the yard, and to carry their eye through every gallery, then like unto ravens where they spy the carrion thither they fly, and press as near as they can . . . giving them pippins . . . dally with their garments to pass the time.' The

36

* Ten or eleven times more in our money.

The Globe Theatre

Controversy still rages as to what the first and second Globe theatres looked like—and, indeed, as to which of the two theatres is represented by early engravings. Most of these are minute, sketchy and much of the evidence is contradictory. The best indication we have as to what the exterior of the second Globe looked like comes from a drawing by Hollar representing London in the 1640's. (We have no very precise details as to what the exterior of the first Globe looked like, most earlier assumptions have been recently discredited.) (*Copyright Iolo A. Williams*)

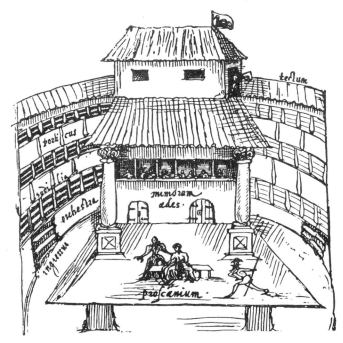

Elizabethan theatre interior

This drawing of the Swan Theatre, *c.* 1596, is the only visual record we have as to what the interior of any of the Elizabethan theatres looked like. Known as the 'de Witt' sketch, it is not even the original sketch (which has not come to light) but a copy made by a friend for his common-place book. De Witt's letter on London theatres was also copied and tells us that the Swan was 'the largest and most distinguished . . . it has space for 3,000 persons' (i.e. nearly half as much again as a present-day giant theatre like Drury Lane)

women take 'such care for their garments, that they be not trod on: such eyes to their laps . . . such pillows to their backs, that they take no hurt: such masking in their ears, I know not what'. 'There is such tickling, such toying, such smiling, such winking, and such manning them home, when the sports are ended, that it is right comedy to mark their behaviour.' The youths and idle apprentices 'fight for bitten apples'. 'Fruits, such as apples, pears and nuts, according to the season, are carried about to be sold, as well as wine and ale.' The stage-keeper can be seen 'gathering up the broken apples for the bears within'. 'Aged fathers' sit 'knee-deep in nutshells.' 'At these spectacles and everywhere else, the English are constantly smoking . . . tobaca' in 'pipes on purpose made of clay.' Even the women take a puff as the pipe is passed from mouth to mouth. 'Lighting it, they draw the smoke into their mouths, which they puff out again through their nostrils, like funnels.' The people in the lower gallery that juts onto the turmoil of the yard are protected from the scuffling by 'iron pikes' set in the surrounding parapet. If you are a foolish young gallant, dressed like 'feathered ostrich', you may 'have a good stool for sixpence'* and sit on the stage itself, or, if the stools be all gone, pay to lie 'on the very rushes where the comedy is to dance . . . beating down the mews and hisses of the opposed rascality . . . neither are you to be hunted from thence, though the scarecrows in the yard hoot at you, hiss at you, spit at you, yea throw dirt even in your teeth'. Perhaps your pocket is picked (and the cut-purse caught and tied to a post on the stage long kept there for that purpose). Perhaps 'you fall to cards . . . to gull the ragamuffins that stand aloof gaping at you, throw the cards, having first torn four or five of them, round about the stage . . . salute all your gentle acquaintance, that are spread either on the rushes, or on stools about you . . . . Take up a rush and tickle the earnest ears of your fellow gallants, to make fools fall a-laughing.' Or perhaps you wander the stage to read 'the pretty stories' painted like tapestries on the 'coarse hangings' through which just now 'the half-dress'd player peep'd to see how the house did fill' or throw pears against the curtains to allure the players forth.

Now 'the quaking Prologue hath by rubbing got colour into his cheeks, and is ready to give the trumpets their cue that he is upon point to enter'. The trumpet calls three times and a hush falls over the busy throng as Prologue, in his black robes, prays 'the company that's in to hear them patiently'. Into the 'gorgeous', 'sumptuous' painted beauty of the playhouse and its stage, colour floods as the players enter 'most expensively and elegantly apparelled (since it is customary . . . when distinguished gentlemen or knights die, for nearly the finest of their clothes to be . . . given to their servants' who 'give them to the comedians to purchase for a small sum').

The players tell their tale. In 'stately speeches and well-sounding phrases' we are shown, perhaps 'The twelve labours of *Hercules* . . . terribly thundered. . . . Hercules hunting the boare, knocking downe the bull, taming the hart, fighting with Hydra, murdering Geryon, slaughtering Diomed, wounding the Stymphalides, Killing the Centaurs, pashing the lion, squeezing the dragon . . . oh, these were the sights'. Or 'three scenes of the devil on the highway to heaven'. Or 'Hector all besmered in blood, trampling upon the bulkes of kinges; Troilus returning from the field . . . as if man and horse, even from the steed's rough fetlockes to the plume on the champion's helmet, had bene together plunged into a

38
* Ten or eleven times more in our money.

Reconstruction of the Globe Theatre for Shakespeare's *Henry V*, with Sir Laurence Olivier. **Inside the Globe Theatre**
(*Copyright Rank Organization*)

purple ocean'. 'Sometimes you shall see nothing but the adventures of an amorous knight, passing from countrie to countrie for the love of his lady encountring many a terrible monster made of brown paper.'

A bare minimum of scenery suffices for all are accustomed to piece out the scenic imperfections with their thoughts. A few words suffice to conjure up 'many days and many places. . . . Asia of the one side, and Afric of the other, and so many other under-kingdoms that the player when he cometh in, must ever begin with telling where he is. . . . Now he shall have three ladies walk to gather flowers and then we must believe the stage to be a garden. But there behind, we hear news of a shipwreck in the same place, and then we are to blame if we accept it not for a rock. Upon the back of that, comes out a hideous monster with fire and smoke, and then the miserable beholders are bound to take it for a cave. While in the meantime, two armies fly in, represented with four swords and bucklers and then what hard heart will not receive it for a pitched field'.

Sometimes a 'creaking throne comes downe, the boys to please' from the 'painted heavens' of the stage roof, 'the garret where perchance Jove lies leaning on his elbows, or is employed to make squibs and crackers to grace the play'—Jove's thunderbolt. Bullets are rolled 'to say, it thunders' and 'tempestuous drumme rumbles, to tell you when the storm doth come'. Sometimes the actor introduces 'novelties and strange trifles to content the vain humours of his rude auditors, faining countries never heard of; monsters and prodigious creatures that are not; as of the Arimaspie, of the Grips, the Pigmeies, the Cranes and other such notorious lies'.

In Tragedie the 'Actors are Goddes, Goddesses, Furies, Fyends, Hagges, Kings, Queens or Potentates'. In Commedie 'whores, queans, bawdes, scullions, knaves, Curtezans, lecherous old men, amorous young men, with such like of infinite variety'. The player also 'sendeth in Gearish apparell, maskes, vaulting, tumbling, daunsing of gigges, galiardes, morisces, hobbihorses'.

'In the pauses of the comedy food and drink are carried round amongst the people, and one can thus refresh himself at his cost.' 'The tobacco-men . . . walk up and down, selling for a penny-pipe, that which was not worth twelve-pence a horseload.'

Some there are who say of the plays 'that to chaste ears they are as odious, as filthy pictures are offensive to modest eyes . . . scratching the itching humours of scabbed minds with pleasing content and profane jests', using 'execrable oaths, artificial lies . . . scurrilous words, obscene discourses, corrupt courtings, licentious motions, lascivious actions, and lewd jestures'. (Certainly the 'playhouse book-keeper when the actors miss their entrance . . . would swear like an elephant and stamp and stare [God bless us]'.) Others say, with the playwright Nashe, that plays 'show the ill-success of treason, the fall of hasty climbers, the wretched end of usurpers, the misery of civil dissension, and how just God is evermore in punishing murder'. Plays anatomize 'most lively . . . all cozenages, all cunning drifts over-gilded with outward holiness . . . all the canker-worms that breed on the rust of peace'.

The actor that is commendable, 'doth not strive to make nature monstrous . . . she (nature) is oft seene in the same scaene with him, but neither on Stilts nor Crutches; and for his voice tis not lower than the prompter, nor lowder than the Foile and Target. Of all men living, a worthy Actor . . . is the strongest motive of affection that can be: for when he dies, we cannot be perswaded any man can do his parts like him'.

In a few hours the player 'runs through the world: marries, gets children, makes children men, men to conquer kingdoms, murder monsters, and bringeth Gods from Heaven and fetcheth Devils from Hell'. The play is 'concluded with variety of dances, accompanied by excellent music'. The 'epilogue says "clap or crown"' and earns 'the excessive applause of those that are present', 'the tag-rag people clap', 'peasants ope their throats', 'youths thunder' and 'the rude, rascal rabble cry "excellent, excellent".'

The composite picture assembled above is made up of extracts taken from many contemporary sources. It includes only such material as could, with sensible freedom, be attributed to performances *c*. 1600—three years before Elizabeth died. Each single quotation is authentic but their combined effect may contain some distortion. It is the exceptional that gets recorded—and the picturesque that one is most tempted to select. The general impression that one gets, for example, of the audience as boisterous and inattentive may well be an exaggerated picture. The information comes mostly from pamphlets, the newspapers of their day. A few of these are written by journalists, more concerned with a colourful story than a true picture; the majority by interested parties, both hotly partisan.

The playwrights are too fulsome in defence of the theatre and too concernedly, too satirically censorious of the inattentive few in the audience. The priests are too violent in their attacks, seeing the theatre as 'The Devil's Chapel' and are so bigoted that they would have had Shakespeare for ever silenced because whores were touting among his audience. We must throw into the balance the calmer voice of an impartial foreign visitor who records an audience 'listening as silently and soberly as possible'. Even this we must qualify for the date of the comment is 1617, Elizabeth and Shakespeare are both dead, and the theatre is seventeen years older than that portrayed in our picture and perhaps wiser and better-behaved.

The Elizabethan Theatre

Shakespeare in Elizabeth's Time The known facts of Shakespeare's life are few. He was born in Stratford in 1564. At eighteen he was forced to marry Anne Hathaway, a girl of twenty-six he had got with child. His daughter Susanna was born six months later in 1583 and the twins nearly two years later, Hamnet, the son (who died when he was eleven) and the second daughter, Judith. Shakespeare was then twenty-one. He is twenty-eight when he is next heard of, established in London as actor and dramatist. At thirty he appeared as joint payee with Burbage and Kempe for sums received for playing at Court by the Chamberlain's men, and can be assumed to have advanced to some prominence. At thirty-three he neglected to pay his taxes on his London home in Bishopsgate, but purchased the freehold of New Place in Stratford. At thirty-five he had moved his London quarters to Bankside, near to the newly opened Globe, of which he was a shareholder. At thirty-eight, he is rich enough to buy for £320* the freehold of Combe, some 127 acres at Old Stratford.

Shakespeare began as an actor. His abilities as a writer first showed themselves in im-

* Ten or eleven times more in our money.

Shakespeare

The Frontispiece to the First Folio, 1623, is the only reliable pictorial evidence that we have as to what Shakespeare looked like. (*Author's collection*)

proving the plays of others (*Henry VI—the 3 parts*). This early 'prentice period shows him alternating between the histories and explorations in comedy. It shows him, too, indebted to familiar models; the voices of his predecessors are everywhere. The Old Chronicle plays he transmutes into the great cycle of the Histories. The voice of Kyd's *Spanish Tragedy* can be heard echoing in *Richard III* (*c.* 1593) though Shakespeare subtly leavens his melodrama with sardonic humour. Marlowe's *Edward II* is echoed in *Richard II* (*c.* 1595)—and his mastery of the blank verse line everywhere. The old Classical comedies dictate the form and much of the manner of *The Comedy of Errors* (*c.* 1592) and *The Taming of the Shrew* (*c.* 1593). Lyly's elegance is as much imitated in *Love's Labour's Lost* (*c.* 1594) as it is gently parodied. (The Italian clown-characters of the *Commedia dell'Arte* bustle about in all the early plays.) The first fledgling tragedy, *Romeo and Juliet* (*c.* 1595) foreshadows the majesty to come. Between this and *Julius Caesar* (1599), he achieves his sovereignty over comedy in *A Midsummer Night's Dream*, *Twelfth Night*, *As You Like It* and *Much Ado about Nothing*. Ben Jonson testified to Elizabeth's liking for Shakespeare's work and there is a tradition that 'she was so well pleased with that admirable character of Falstaff' as it had appeared in *Henry IV* (*c.* 1597) that she commended 'one play more, and to shew him in love', as the poet did in *The Merry Wives of Windsor* (*c.* 1600). The dying years of Elizabeth's reign see Shakespeare working on the first of the major tragedies—*Hamlet*—and established at the head of his profession. Fifteen of his plays have been published and more must have been performed, roughly half his total output; but his greatest work still lies ahead.*

* See Theatre of James I for continuation, p. 45.

The Dramatic Workshop In the time of Shakespeare and his successors there were not enough people in London to support a play for a long run. A very successful play might be given once a week in its first season, but the majority only had a very few performances. There was thus always an urgent need for new plays and, as writing for the theatres paid better than any other form of writing, there grew to be a large body of writers able to provide plays at short notice. Writer 1 submits a short summary of an intended play to a company of players. If approved, this may be passed to Writer 2 who is commissioned to write the main plot on condition that he gets Writer 3 to write the sub-plot. If either Writers 2 or 3 are especially busy, they may hand over a scene or two to Writers 4 and 5. A few sheets at a time are sent to the players as soon as they are ready. If sufficient scenes are not arriving to time, or if the early samples seem poorly written, Writer 6 may be introduced to hasten or refurbish the work. Writer 7 may be asked to knock the whole thing into shape for trial by performance.

It was by no means out of the ordinary for a new play to be commissioned to be ready within a fortnight. What better way of hastening the work than to ask Dekker to handle the low-life scenes of the sub-plot, Heywood the two middle-class scenes, Ford (if you can't get Webster) the assorted horrors and murders, and retain Massinger to give the whole thing some shape and order? (Incidentally, very similar methods are used by present-day film and television companies.) In some instances, there is evidence of one each of five acts of a play being given to five different dramatists to write. Few Jacobean playwrights would object to such arrangements for they were common practice. Chambers states that of one hundred and thirty new plays recorded by manager Henslowe, well over half were written in collaboration by from two to as many as five hands. And who knows how many of the plays recorded as by a single hand were written in collaborations of which Henslowe was not advised? The dramatists had little pride of ownership in their plays and seldom troubled to oversee the printing of their work because the entire copyright passed to the players once the writers had been paid 'in full'. (The dramatists were given a small sum 'on account' as retainer, further driblets as further sheets arrived and paid 'in full' only on delivery of the final written text. The total sums paid ranged from £4 to £10* during Elizabeth's reign, rising later to between £10 and £20,* plus an occasional bonus for successful plays of 'the overplus of the second day', that is, the profits.)

These conditions lead to great difficulties when it comes to ascribing plays to their true authors. *Titus Andronicus* is nowadays included in the collected works of Shakespeare on little better ground than that it appeared in the Folio of 1623, the first published collected works, assembled by his friends and fellow-actors, Heminge and Condell, seven years after Shakespeare's death. Reputable modern scholarship allows only a bare minimum of *Titus* to be Shakespeare's work. *Sir Thomas More* is not included in most collected works of Shakespeare, yet many reputable scholars allow him to be one of the five discernible authors. The collected works of Beaumont and Fletcher published in 1647 credit them with the joint authorship of fifty-three plays—modern scholarship credits the partnership with only six or seven plays. The great bulk are attributed either to other dramatists, or to Fletcher singly, or in double harness with Massinger and others.

* Ten or eleven times more in our money.

Furthermore there was always a discrepancy between the Author's copy and the Acted text (often used for printing). The Acted text would be a strange hotch-potch with lines cut or altered to meet or forestall the objections of the Censor, cut or altered to suit the players, cut to save the expense of an extra small-part actor, altered to include topical references, or refurbished to suit special occasions. In some cases, where the master copies were lost when the theatre was burnt, the Acted text would be reassembled by calling in the actors' written parts for the purpose. There is barely a play of the period that does not present us with problems, either of authorship or text. It is the Shakespearean plays that have attracted the major share of scholarship and research. When all the other dramatists have received a similar wealth of attention, who knows what reshuffling of authors will be justified? There can be few plays that any properly cautious scholar would attribute solely to one hand. Of fewer still can we be sure that in the printed form left to us have we any certain reproduction of the author's original intentions—let alone what text he would have left to posterity had he himself thought it worthwhile to supervise any definitive edition.

CHAPTER FOUR

The Theatre of James I and Charles I

England's world changed drastically when Elizabeth died and James I came to the throne in 1603. Elizabeth had inherited a divided country but, though many factions bitterly opposed each other throughout her long reign, she and her advisers contrived to hold her society in balance. The splendid motley team moved forward because the Queen knew how to play them with the loose rein of a measured diplomacy. James was no diplomat—the horses bucked, the reins broke, and the carriage of state fetched up with its near wheels in the ditch.

However disparate the factions beneath her, Elizabeth had found little difficulty in achieving a national unity so long as there was a threat of invasion from Spain. Within a year of coming to the throne, James made peace with Spain. The threat of invasion gone, the nation's unity had gone; the factions were let loose and, as the reign proceeded, the seeds of Civil War were sown. Another year passed, and the new King provoked three conspiracies. Catholics attempted to blow up both King and Parliament. Three hundred Puritan ministers gave up their livings rather than accept the King's dictum that he was established on his throne by the will of God. The people lost their rights to liberty of speech, Parliament lost the right to control its own elections, seven of the people's representatives were accused of treason and imprisoned for attempting to prevent the King from usurping these traditional rights. Denied the freedom to worship in their own way or to be governed in ways of their own choosing, Englishmen began to leave their country, boat-load after boat-load finding their way to the continent and, eventually, setting out to make a new life for themselves in America.

Elizabeth's common sense was superseded by James's common sensuality. The Queen had had advisers; James had favourites. She had contrived to weld a unity out of diversity by expedient or tolerant compromise. Too headstrong for expedience or tolerance, James

45

was unable to compromise. He alienated himself from his parliament, his priests and his people, and withdrew into an ever-narrowing circle of sycophantic and profligate court favourites. James exacerbated almost every available sore on the body politic and his proud intellect explored whole new worlds of intolerance.

Despite the immediate and drastic change of atmosphere, the theatre had, however, acquired such a colossal momentum under Elizabeth that its major figure, at least, was temporarily able to withstand the new pressures.

With the accession of James, Shakespeare at thirty-nine was poised to mount his own throne. Now came the great succession of major tragedies that followed upon *Hamlet*. With *Othello* (*c.* 1604), *Lear* (*c.* 1605), *Macbeth* (*c.* 1606) and *Antony and Cleopatra* (*c.* 1607) his genius was in full spate. The apprenticeship was over; the echoes of others were less and less predominant: more and more each play was a mutation from his own early work. If he felt the pressure from the troubled world outside, this had no power to interrupt the majestic flow of his work . . . yet.

In the first year of James's reign, Shakespeare and Burbage with their company became the King's men under royal patent and it was they who dominated the early years of James's theatre. (In the first thirteen years of the reign, they gave 177 performances at court, far more than the total given by all other companies.)

Three years after James came to the throne, the first of Ben Jonson's best plays, *Volpone*, was produced. *The Silent Woman* (*Epicoene*), *The Alchemist* and *Bartholomew Fair* followed respectively in three, four and eight years. Jonson was born eight years

The theatres under King James

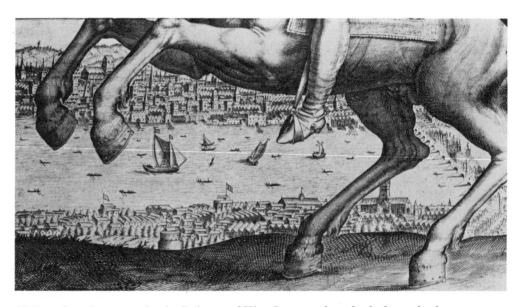

This section of an engraving by Delaram of King James on horseback shows, in the background, an interesting view of the theatres on Bankside, the Bear-Garden, the Rose and the first Globe. It shows the city as it was when James came to the throne in 1603. (*Copyright Windsor Castle Library*)

Ben Jonson

Honthorst's fine portrait serves as model for this engraving
by Vertue and many others that followed. It is sad that we
have no portrait of Shakespeare that is equally revealing.
(*Author's collection*)

later than Shakespeare. Their paths ran parallel; but their characters, lives and work were
in sharp contrast. Shakespeare is remembered as 'gentle'; Jonson was savage, a hostile
satirist and contentious reformer. Shakespeare's public life was of so little event as to be
enigmatic; Jonson's was turbulent, full of wrangles and protests (he was imprisoned three
times for outspoken plays and once for killing a man). Shakespeare quietly evolved his own
drama of people and seldom wandered into theory; Jonson retained the old 'type' characters
of the Moralities within his device of 'humours' and hurtled into a war of words, a battle
fought out in plays for supremacy in the domain of style. There is little that is merely
topical in Shakespeare's plays; Jonson's give us a vivid caricature of contemporary life.
Shakespeare held the mirror up to that in nature which is eternal; Jonson tied current
cranks and knaves to the whipping-post and lashed hard. His bounteous and abundant
vitality made him cussedly independent of any authority that he did not choose to recognize
as valid and, for a time, energetic in his censure of the ever-growing corruption. He lived
hard, worked hard, attacked fearlessly and gave generously. (It is to him that we turn for
praise of his worthiest fellows.) As we think of Jonson thwacking about him, we do well
to remember that the times demanded forthright, energetic people—and that he was
'nobly wild, not mad'.

For sixteen years, from his early *Every Man in his Humour* in 1598 (in which Shakespeare is said to have acted Knowell) to *Bartholomew Fair* in 1614, Jonson's concern was
almost wholly with comedy. In 1600 he had included a Masque in *Cynthia's Revels*.

47

An Elizabethan
masque

A painting of *Sir Henry Unton's Wedding*, *c.* 1597, in the National Portrait Gallery, which portrays vividly the disposition of performers and audience and gives one some idea of the atmosphere of an Elizabethan masque. (*Copyright National Portrait Gallery*)

Masques were increasingly in favour at court and Jonson was poor and anxious to become Poet Laureate. This post he eventually occupied from 1619 to his death in 1637, most of which time he spent in writing Masques.

By Elizabeth's time the Masque (which had its origins with the early Mummers) had evolved into a court entertainment. Masques were acted by courtiers in compliment to the Queen and featured rich costumes, a multiplicity of scenic devices, much music and less verse, and culminated in a dance in which the performers mingled with the spectators. Under James, the Masque pursued even greater splendours. The quarry was, on occasion, elusive; Sir John Harington gives a joyful description of a Masque given to honour the King of Denmark's visit to James's court in 1606. 'A great feast was held, and, after dinner, the representation of Solomon his Temple and the coming of the Queen of Sheba was made, or (as I may better say) was meant to have been made, before their Majesties. . . . The Lady who did play the Queen's part . . . forgetting the steppes arising to the canopy, overset her caskets into his Danish Majesties lap, and fell at his feet, tho I rather think it was in his face. Much was the hurry and confusion; cloths and napkins were at hand to make all clean. His Majesty then got up and would dance with the Queen of Sheba; but he fell down and humbled himself before her, and was carried to an inner chamber, and laid on a bed of state; which was not a little defiled with the presents of the Queen which had been bestowed on his garments; such as wine, cream, jelly, beverage, cakes, spices and other good matters. The entertainment and show went forward, and most of the presenters went backward, or fell down; wine did so occupy their upper chambers. Now did appear, in rich dress, Hope, Faith, and Charity: Hope did assay to speak, but wine rendered her endeavours so feeble that she withdrew, and hoped the King would excuse her brevity: Faith . . . left the court in a staggering condition: Charity . . . in some sorte made obeysance . . . then returned to Hope and Faith, who were both sick and spewing in the lower hall. . . . Victory . . . after much lamentable utterance . . . was laid to sleep in in the outer steps of the ante-chamber. Now did Peace make entry, and strive to get foremoste to the King; . . . and, much contrary to her semblance, most rudely made war with her olive branch, and laid on the pates of those who did oppose her coming.' These merry ladies were all courtiers. (There were, of course, no actresses yet in the public theatres.) Acting had become a fashionable way of killing time among the nobility. Even James, the King, on one occasion allowed himself to be lowered from the heavens in a stage machine.

Shakespeare was forty-four and James had been on the throne for five years when the Shakespeare-Burbage company took over the Blackfriars theatre, hitherto ostensibly a private theatre. Roofed over and more intimate in atmosphere, the Blackfriars was used more and more by the Company, particularly in winter. The actors got 'more in one winter . . . by a thousand pounds* than they were used to get on Bankside'. They charged higher prices and their audiences entirely changed character. Elizabeth's theatre had welcomed men from all walks of life; the noble man and the common man rubbed shoulders in the playhouse yard; and the span of each play's interest held matter for them both. Five years after James came to the throne, the nobility and the people went separate ways. The latter went to the Red Bull and other houses where the fare was simple. The nobility went

The Theatre of James I and Charles I

* Ten or eleven times more in our money.

49

indoors to the bright lights of the 'private' theatre at Blackfriars, where the players found their living depended on satisfying more rarefied appetites.

James's dark court becomes the nature to which the dramatists must hold up the mirror. Even the gentle, temperate Shakespeare is thrown off balance. He enters the dark period of his writing. In a story that broods on the ills that men and women of no tolerance do to each other, and on the dangers of trusting unworthy confidants, a King usurps a young noble's right to choose his own wife, leaving him no alternative but to leave his country. The bitter comedy is called *All's Well that Ends Well*. 'Man, proud man, Drest in a little brief authority, Most ignorant of what he's most assured . . . Plays such fantastic tricks before high heaven, As makes the angels weep.' The fantastic tricks are tricks of intolerance; the intolerance of a clever man for thoughtless people: the intolerance of a chaste Puritan girl for the 'gross body's treason' that stirs in amoral youth. In the absence of a true sovereign, a kingdom where lust, treachery and murder flourish is ruled by a clever, intolerant, unworthy deputy. The one tolerant man of his times, the true sovereign, returns in disguise to expose heartless cleverness and render a judgement that allows just *Measure for Measure*. A proud noble seeks rule over a people that he despises, convinced that that honour is due to him by the divine right of aristocratic birth. Rejected, he allies himself with his country's traditional enemy; invades and conquers his own land; betrays his true allies: and is accused of treason to a country that was never rightly his. Conspirators kill *Coriolanus*. A noble man gives all he has to his fellow countrymen but his friends prove to be parasites and reward him only with ingratitude. Bitterness leads this gentle man to rail in hate at a world grown so degenerate. He withdraws, first into the seclusion of the countryside, and finally into the only mercy left for him, death. *Timon of Athens* was written as Shakespeare's mind was turning to thoughts of his own retirement from James's world—and all four plays within the first five years of James's reign. In part they reflect the disturbed times, in part the fatigue that comes upon a writer after a prolonged spell of major work. The dramatist, it seems, is holding up the fairground's distorting mirror to nature—but in truth it is not the mirror that is distorted but the times themselves that are out of joint.

Seven years after James comes to the throne, Shakespeare, now forty-six, returns to Stratford, where he writes less and less. A master of words, secure in his isolation, so indulges his magic intellect that it attracts to him all the intriguers and usurpers who inhabit the stormy world he has left behind. Not until he has revealed their true natures to them do they believe in the sovereign power of this magician. It is this power alone which can guide them safely across troubled seas to a country left without a true monarch. *The Tempest* written, Shakespeare-Prospero goes home—'thought is free'. At forty-nine, he writes no more; for three years his affairs are those of the family and the peaceful countryside of his native Stratford. In 1616 at the age of fifty-two 'Shakespeare, Drayton and Ben Jonson, had a merry meeting, and it seems drank too hard, for Shakespeare died of a fever there contracted'. So the Vicar of Stratford some forty-six years later records the tradition. 'The little that was mortal of Shakespeare'* lies buried in Stratford Church.

* The phrase is that of Professor Chambers, whose researches into the Elizabethan theatre and Shakespeare's life leave all scholars gratefully in his debt.

In 1613 Burbage's company were acting at the Globe the new play of Henry VIII when the stage guns set fire to the thatched roof and the 'virtuous fabric' suffered a 'fatal period'. Within a year the theatre was 'new builded in far fairer manner than before' (with a roof of tiles) at a total cost of some £1,600* which the actors were able to find themselves. That they were rich enough to do so indicates the popularity that the theatre had been enjoying. Elizabeth's court had seen sixty-seven plays in forty-five years. James and his court see more than four times as many in only the first thirteen years of his reign. Eight years after the Globe was burnt down, the Fortune Theatre (built some twenty years earlier) 'the fayrest playhouse in this towne . . . was quite burnt downe in two howres, and all their apparell & play-bookes lost, whereby those poore companions are quite undone'.

The Puritans, inevitably, saw the hand of a vengeful God in 'the sudden fearful burning, even to the ground, both of the Globe and Fortune playhouses, no man perceiving how these fires came'. Prynne wrote this in *Histriomastix* (1633) with much more about 'devil's chapels' (the theatres); and his was only one of many Puritan voices raised against the players. So fierce is their invective and so knowledgeable do they show themselves of the vices attendant upon the theatres that we are driven to think, as Charles Lamb did many years later, 'Have we never heard an old preacher in the pulpit display such an insight into the mystery of ungodliness as made us wonder how a good man came by it.' Not all of their objections, however, were unreasonable. The Plague was a constant threat to Londoners and those who swelled the crowds at the theatres courted grave danger from infection.

In 1642 Civil War, long imminent, at last broke out. An Order of Parliament decreed 'Whereas public sports doe not well agree with public calamities . . . public stage-playes . . . being spectacles of pleasure too commonly expressing lascivious mirth and levitie . . . shall cease and be forborne.' Five years later a further edict threatened actors playing in 'stage-plays, interludes or other common playes' with imprisonment and punishment as rogues. A year after that yet another edict decreed the punishment of all players 'whether wanderers or no, notwithstanding any licence whatsoever from the King or any person'. Further, all places where plays were acted were to be demolished and all spectators fined.

Shakespeare's Rivals and Successors Posterity has so firmly established Shakespeare as supreme that it is salutary to remember that Jacobean judgement regarded Beaumont and Fletcher as his superiors and that this remained the predominant attitude for some hundred years to come.

The drama of the period resolves itself into two main categories—plays that reflect the Court's taste and those that keep alive the more lasting traditions of the people's theatre. The mere titles of the plays are sufficient to indicate the contrast between the two influences. *The Shoemaker's Holiday, A Woman Killed with Kindness, The Fair Maid of the West, The English Traveller* and *May Day* all sound sweetly and speak for the popular taste. *If It Be Not Good, the Devil's In It* warns Dekker, and from there on the devil's in

* Ten or eleven times more in our money.

it with a vengeance as the Court's taste darkens: *The Honest Whore*, *'Tis Pity She's a Whore*, *The Revenger's Tragedy*, *The Atheist's Tragedy*, *The Rape of Lucrece*, *The White Devil*, *The Roaring Girl*, *The City Madam*, *The Woman Hater* and *Women Beware Women*. There is a kind of finality about *All's Lost by Lust* but perhaps the last words should go to *All Fools* and *A Mad World, My Masters*.

As time goes on, less and less plays are written for the open-air public theatres, and more and more for the indoor theatres that serve the Court and fashionable audiences. It is the Court that the Players and their writers must please if they are to live. Shakespeare had mastered his times. The Jacobean Court dramatists are content to master their market—and they pay the penalty by becoming the slaves of their time. The Court prove themselves gluttons for excitement and, as their palates grow more jaded, the dramatists are forced to ever-increasing extremes. Perhaps the heart of the trouble is that the King had no conscience that a play could catch—only an appetite that novel and exotic sensations could tease. Under his influence the human story degenerates into a mere play-plot, its people into attitudinizing puppets, and a love of life into no more than a titillation of the senses. The country finds its Pym and others who stand out against the King's tyrannies. The theatre, except for a few isolated gestures, gives in and surrenders its house to the King's caprice. (And we are left to ponder how the great galaxy of dramatists would have fared under better influences.)

Tourneur has fifteen or more deaths in *The Atheist's Tragedy* and this is only one example among many that labour under the delusion that six murders in one play make it twice as exciting as one play with three murders, twelve murders four times as exciting, and so on *ad absurdem*. Soon no play is complete without its heap of corpses on the stage at curtain-fall. Swinburne neatly describes the disease when he refers to the blood-bath at the end of Middleton's *Women Beware Women* as 'solution by massacre'. Six people die in less than six pages. Livia causes Isabella to die of the vapour from poisoned incense; but is incautious enough to catch a whiff of it herself; the Duke dies from drinking poison prepared by his wife for his brother, the Cardinal; the Duchess then drinks what is left; Hippolito is shot (by Cupid) with a poisoned arrow, then runs on the sword of a guard. Guardiano stamps on the floor and falls through a trap onto a board-full of iron spikes that he has prepared for another. The Duke is a lecherous voluptuary; Leantio is adulterous; Hippolito is incestuous; Guardino is a pander and murderous; Isabella is adulterous and incestuous; Livia is adulterous and murderous. And so on. Of the main characters, only one, the Cardinal, is good—and he alone is left alive to moralize over the corpses. 'Sin, what thou art, these ruins show too piteously etc.' All this is silly enough stuff, but there is much in the play that is not. Nor is this play exceptional. Bathos haunts the purple-passageway beside the Jacobean playhouse and is forever gate-crashing its more flamboyant celebrations:

> A woman dipped in blood and talk of modesty!
> How the turtle pants. . . .
> By this warm, reeking gore, I'll marry her!
> Poison the father, butcher the son and marry the mother, ha!

This is not one speech from one play but four separate lines from two plays by different authors; much of the dialogue in these horror dramas is equally sad, interchangeable, all-purpose stuff. A less random choice from the plays reminds us that all is not sound and fury told in moments of idiocy:

> But now 'tis night, and a long night with her. . . .

says Shirley's Florio of his dead sister. And when the Duke kisses the dead girl the dramatist reveals the same sure touch:

> What winter dwells upon this lip. . . .

We may regret that Ford's:

> I would not change this minute for Elysium. . . .

has to grace a scene of incest but the grace is, nevertheless, truly there.

There are moments of deathless beauty dotted about all over the graveyard drama of the times. Too often, alas, when the sublime gesture is made, the ridiculous is at hand, jogging the elbow. Few creatures die a single death for two stabs are always thought better than one—and a mixed death (poison *and* strangulation) must be better than either. It is a strange country of wolfish men and strained white-wanton women where violence and betrayal, murder, adultery, rape, and incest are commonplace. Ghosts and witches haunt, twitch and cackle under veiled moons and whole cataracts of heavenly thunderbolts. Swords seem to strain at the necks of their scabbards, chalices to spout poison involuntarily, and every rope loops unbidden to a noose. Rings are poisoned, crowns are poisoned, skulls are dressed to the life, veins are opened, tongues are torn out, tongues are nailed to the stage, severed hands are passed round, limbs of children are offered on salvers, bleeding trunks of slaughtered men are bound to children's bodies—these are the dainty dishes set before the King. The plays leave the normal walks of life and enter a hot-house atmosphere of forced growths, unnatural graftings, proliferating artifice and a dizzying over-luxuriance that leaves us gasping for air. In the end it is the Property-master, with his ever-ready bowls of blood and assorted severed limbs, who becomes the main protagonist. When everything so desperately attempts to be surprising, nothing surprises any more—though much may shock. It was 'painting and carpentry' that drove Ben Jonson to leave the Masque. A less literal (but more dangerous) over-painting in the verse and over-carpentry in the plots of the Jacobean dramatists rob them of life. (Play-carpenters make only skeletons; play-makers clothe the bare bones in flesh and blood.)

Beaumont and Fletcher are chiefly remembered for their least typical play, one written for the ordinary playhouse people in the early days of their collaboration*—*The Knight of the Burning Pestle*. Its honest freshness is quite unlike anything that they write later under

---

* Collaboration was the order of the day. Many of the plays in this section that are assigned to their major author are the work of more than one hand (see The Dramatic Workshop, page 43).

The Theatre of James I and Charles I

Shakespeare's rivals and successors

(1) Francis Beaumont, from an engraving by Vertue, 1711
(2) John Fletcher, from an engraving by Vertue, 1711
(3) Thomas Dekker (from an anonymous woodcut)
(4) George Chapman, from an engraving by J. T. Wedgwood, 1820, taken from the portrait by J. Thurston
(5) Thomas Middleton, from an engraving by C. Rolls, 1821, taken from the portrait by J. Thurston
(6) Philip Massinger, from an engraving by J. Cross, 1623 (*With the exception of* (3) *which is the copyright of the Mander and Mitchenson Theatre Collection, the rest are the copyright of the National Portrait Gallery*)

the Court's malevolent influence. Beaumont was the son of a Justice, Fletcher of a Bishop. Both had university educations; both became well versed in the ways of the Court. Under their influence, the theatre further extends its preoccupation with manner rather than with matter, with style rather than with human conduct. Like many of their contemporaries, they prove themselves prolific and versatile, writing burlesques, pastorals, romantic tragicomedies, melodramas, farces and an epic tragedy or two. They find themselves best suited to romantic comedy, where their exuberance and the grace of their verse enlivens such plots as are not too ostentatiously well-knit. *Rule a Wife and Have a Wife*, perhaps the best of these, and the more farcical *The Wild-Goose Chase*, centre round the exploits of Gallants whose guile and cavalier charm make easy conquests of women. Though the artificial and complicated manoeuvring of the plots, the wrenching-in of too theatrical sensationalism, prevents our believing in what the people of the Beaumont and Fletcher plays do, we can often find much pleasure in what they say. Hear them talk on death in *Philaster* :

> 'Tis less than to be born; a lasting sleep;
> A quiet resting from all jealousy,
> A thing we all pursue. . . .
> It is but giving over of a game
> That must be lost

on death and drinking in *The Bloody Brother* :

> And he that will to bed go sober,
> Falls with the leaf still in October.

on life stirring in a happy virgin in *The Faithful Shepherdess* :

> For from one cause of fear I am most free:
> It is impossible to ravish me,
> I am so willing. . . .

Three of their colleagues—Dekker, Heywood and Chapman—remain predominantly on the side of the angels, though their reasons for this differ greatly. Dekker is said to have begun as a tailor's apprentice and, clearly, his world is that of the cockney back streets. 'Honest labour bears a lovely face' he says and he shows an attitude rare in his times in his concern for the poor and oppressed, for whom so many of his colleagues can find only a callous ridicule. He gives us the authentic bustle and stir of the good common people of London. The middle-class world finds a voice in Heywood, a country gentleman (most enthusiastically) turned player. He proves himself no tedious dilettante but an industrious professional who, in addition to acting regularly, finds time to have 'either an entire hand, or at least a main finger' in 220 plays. He is one of the mainstays of the Red Bull, which becomes the people's theatre when higher prices and a too exotic programme

55

discourage attendance at Blackfriars. If we need to be reminded that this would have been a golden age of dramatic verse even without Shakespeare, Heywood is amongst the first witnesses to this:

> Oh God, oh God, that it were possible
> To undo things done, to call back yesterday;
> That time could turn up his swift sandy glass,
> To untell the days, and to redeem these hours:
> Or that the sun
> Could, rising from the West, draw his coach backward,
> Take from the account of time so many minutes
> Till he had all these seasons call'd again,
> Those minutes and those actions done in them,
> Even from her first offence, that I might take her
> As spotless as an Angel in my arms,
> But oh: I talk of things impossible,
> And cast beyond the moon. . . . (*A Woman Killed with Kindness*)

Like Heywood and Dekker, Chapman the scholar is 'his own man' and no pander to the Court. This healthy independence is, however, very nearly the sum of all that he shares with them. Educated at (both!) universities, well travelled, he writes from above life, not from within it. He remains, too, always at one intellectual remove from the workaday theatre's common sense. His plots are a little too naïvely classic, his characters a little too consciously epic. His purple passages, so eagerly conceded to the theatrical taste, are nearly always twice too long—(one can imagine him at rehearsals 'C.U.T.—why that?')—and they are often incautiously purple. To borrow from the immortal Ros's idiom, the tender parts are bruised with bathos's baleful bumps. In *Bussy d'Ambois* a twice-stabbed lady is hoisted aloft, where, says Chapman:

> The too huge bias of the world hath swayed
> Her back part upwards, and with that she braves
> This hemisphere. . . .

We are asked to believe, in *The Widow's Tears*, that a disguised husband could co-habit with his wife and remain unrecognized. An endearing stranger to much of life (and more of the theatre), Chapman finds his truest strength in independence, as in the *Tragedy of the Duke of Byron*:

> I will not die
> Like to a clergyman; but like the captain
> That pray'd on horseback, and with sword in hand
> Threatened the sun, commanding it to stand. . . .

A Mad World, My Masters says Middleton in 1606, heralding the many dramatists who plunge out of the world and into madness:

56

> Black spirits and white, red spirits and grey,
> Mingle, mingle, mingle, you that mingle may. (*The Witch*)

A colourful figure in his romantic coat of many patches, Middleton is a great mingler. He mingles with Dekker, Drayton, Munday, Greene and Rowley in collaborations. His plays mingle the Court's taste for salacious horror and the people's taste for comedies of London manners; and he mingles crude farcical sub-plots with main plots of flamboyant tragedy. Finally he damns himself at Court by mingling politics and play-writing in *A Game of Chess* (1624) which satirizes James's unsuccessful attempts to unite English and Spanish royalty. Popular with the people, the play brings heavy punishment from the Court. He writes no more.

Journeyman dramatists are little averse to trying their hand at anything. Middleton and the less memorable Marston, among others, quite cheerfully unlock the door to the charnel-house. Tourneur dashes in and sets up house there. His *Revenger's Tragedy* and *Atheist's Tragedy* come only one and two years after Middleton's *Mad World*. He leaves us only two plays—but a surfeit of horrors. Rape and incest gambol prettily in Tourneur's playground, panders flourish and ghosts are familiars. The charnel-house is well-nigh the standard setting, but the odd graveyard and brothel are thrown in for occasional light relief. Nothing so becomes Tourneur's daffodil touch as the scene where the lecherous Duke, anticipating a toothsome 'assignation', finds the lady's lips those of a well-dressed skull. Kissing this poison, he goes into convulsions and has his tongue nailed to the stage while his wife and son treat us to the love that is only love when it alteration finds. There are about fifteen deaths in the second play, somewhat less in the first (which is not so bad). Tourneur plays enthusiastic Pelion to James's Ossa—and horror is so piled on horror that our own convulsions are never wholly under control. There is nothing left for the figurative; every cupboard has its real skeleton; and when someone says 'Lend me an ear', a still small voice inside all of us says 'Look out or you won't get it back'. Middleton had written from above madness, Tourneur (a civil servant!) writes from within it. Yet he is not master in his own kingdom. He does it more naturally, but Webster, who is to come, does it with a better grace.

Ford, another who has fingers in the great cannibal pie, shows an equal interest in blood and revenge but is not quite Tourneur's peer in diablerie. He is but mad north-north-west and lacks the true mandrake touch. In his own words he is 'a mushroom on whom the dew of heaven drops now and then'. He says *'Tis Pity She's a Whore* and pity is a kind of hood on those who wish to see as well in the dark as Tourneur does. Ford does contrive one major horror 'novelty'—a chair whose mechanical arms close on its victim—but for the most part our risibility is controllable. A man of independent means, Ford can afford time to reflect. He can afford, too, to scorn popular approval—but not the Court's lawless loves. When he follows this fashion, he is betrayed by frenzies a little too well-ordered and verse a little too clean-cut. He lacks Tourneur's pell-mell, neck-or-nothing involvement. It is with relief that we find him turning, in later life, to the more rebellious *Perkin Warbeck*, where he achieves something of the genuine tragic power that has always lain tauntingly just within his reach but never quite within his grasp.

The Theatre of James I and Charles I

57

Webster, alone of this nightmare trio, can wholly still our ridicule. He shares the same dark world of owl-light and shadow, of skulls and dismembered hands, but there is an immediate authority about his speech that lends a majesty even to such lowly subjects:

> Terrify babes, my lord, with painted devils;
> I am past such needless palsy. For your names
> Of whore and murderess, they proceed from you,
> As if a man should spit against the wind;
> The filth returns in's face. . . .
>
> Go, go, brag
> How many ladies you have undone like me.
> Fare you well, sir; let me hear no more of you:
> I had a limb corrupted to an ulcer,
> But I have cut it off; and now I'll go
> Weeping to Heaven on crutches.   (*Duchess of Malfi*)

His verse is often fit to stand by Shakespeare's, even if his people come from an other-world. Shakespeare's creatures were born under the sun, Webster's are exhaled from some deep midnight cauldron. It is under the moon's pocked face that they writhe—a moon that comes more near the earth than she was wont. Their stunted shadows scrabble at the earth for foothold and they seek heat from strange unholy fires. What gives the stories their authority is that they are the poet's wilful dreams, not unsought nightmares. If anyone can reconcile us to the vault-ward tendency of the age, Webster is the man.

> I am now a servant to voluptuousness.
> Wantons of all degrees and fashions, welcome.

so says Massinger, in *The Picture* leaving us to regret that a gentleman should have had to go into service in such a house. He is as good a craftsman as any in the teeming carpenter's shop of the times. If he is less of a poet than others, he is more of a play-maker. His verses do not greatly enrich the anthologies but his plays prove popular with actors and audiences for some two hundred years to come. (They were particularly favoured by Edmund Kean in the early 1800s.)

Shirley's first comedy was performed in the year that Charles I came to the throne. Constant echoes of his predecessors are heard in his verse but his suiting of model to mood has always a welcome appropriateness. His plays typify the changing taste of the times. Under his influence, the wayward violence of Jacobean tragedy gives place to a greater sense of order and good proportion. In his comedies there is much untrussing of men and undoing of women but his open-air rascals, if not precise paragons of virtue, at least enjoy vices less scabrous than those that inhabited the dank writhing undergrowth he inherited.

Davenant was Shakespeare's godson. 'Have a care that you don't take *God's* name in vain' said an elderly fellow-townsman to the eight-year-old boy, scampering from school to welcome the great man who, whether he was his back-stairs father or not, showed him singular kindness. Much of Davenant's story belongs to later times but mention must be made here of *The Wits*, a comedy of grace and charm fit to stand, at least, with the best of Shirley. It is not only in time that Davenant and Shirley stand between the Elizabethan and the Restoration drama; their verse reaches back to Shakespeare and their stories of rake's progresses reach forward to the Restoration comedies.

The Scenery in Public Theatres remained of the simplest nature. The actors performed in front of what we would nowadays call a permanent set, the back wall of the stage. There appears to have been an outer and an inner stage. This latter could be curtained off and no doubt such necessary pieces of furniture as, for example, Desdemona's bed in *Othello* could in this manner be placed and removed. There were also in the back wall at least two doors and above the inner stage a gallery which was no doubt used for the balcony in *Romeo and Juliet*, and the many scenes in the histories where it was necessary for an actor to address people from the battlements. From such internal evidence as stage directions in the printed plays we may infer that a limited amount of scenery sprouted up through the stage-floor 'trap'. In Greene's *Looking Glass* (*c.* 1590) we read that the Magi 'beat the ground, and from under the same rises a brave arbour'. It seems unlikely that the stage trap would be larger than the 6ft. by 2ft. that would comfortably accommodate Ophelia's body or the Witches' cauldron. Or that the 'brave arbour' and such 'houses' as have been conjectured to rise from below the stage would greatly exceed some five feet in height. (This is the probable height of the stage floor above the ground and as the Globe was 'flanked with a ditch, and forced out of a marsh' (Ben Jonson) any very deep excavation seems improbable.) Whatever fresh evidence may arise, it seems unlikely that it will be sufficient to confute the impression given by the playwrights themselves who continually refer to the simplicity of presentation of such scenes and spectacles as are better left to the imagination.

The Theatre of James I and Charles I

Scenery in Court Masques Some idea of the more ambitious scenic adornment of the Masques of this period can be gained from a study of Ben Jonson's *The Masque of Queens* (1609) designed by Inigo Jones in which 'an ugly hell . . . flaming beneath, smoked into the top of the roof . . . at a sound of loud music . . . quite vanished and the whole face of the scene altered . . . in place of it appeared a glorious and magnificent building, figuring the House of Fame in the top of which were discovered the twelve Masquers, sitting upon a throne triumphal . . . circled with all store of light' above which two figures recline on clouds. The Masquers disappear when 'the throne wherein they sat . . . suddenly changed . . . on the turning of the machine'. The revolving stage, which was some twenty feet up at the top of the scenic House, turned and thus enabled the Masquers to descend out of the audience's view and 'then be mounted into three triumphant chariots ready to come forth' through the central arch of the House. The chariots 'triumphing about the stage' were drawn respectively by eagles, griffins and lions, attended by four torch-bearers and trailing captive witches. After songs and dances, the performers (ladies of the Court, including 'the Queen's Majesty herself') 'took out the men' from their audience and danced 'the measures' for an hour or so.

This period sees the introduction into England of (1) the proscenium arch or picture-frame stage; (2) the painted landscape front-curtain which rose and fell on rollers; (3) revolving stages; (4) revolving wing-pieces, painted on both sides; (5) flats (panels) running in grooves; (6) cloud transparencies; (7) perspective views; and (8) elaborate lighting effects. The majority (if not all) of these were introduced by Inigo Jones; and most of them were more in use in court masques than in the public theatres.

Inigo Jones's design for the House of Fame in Ben Jonson's *The Masque of Queens*, 1609—from Designs by Inigo Jones for Masques and Plays at Court by Percy Simpson and C. F. Bell, Walpole and Malone Societies, 1924. (*Devonshire Collection, Chatsworth. Reproduced by Permission of the Trustees of the Chatsworth Settlement*)

The Civil War The theatres were closed in 1642. For eighteen years, until Charles II commenced his reign in 1660, there were no regular performances. The theatre had for long suffered much opposition from the Puritans and it is not surprising that the players, in general, found themselves on the side of the King and Cavaliers. Some few, among them Shakespeare's grand-nephew, Hart, gained distinction fighting in the Royalist ranks. For the most part, as a newspaper of 1654 has it, 'the poor actors' debarred 'during this long winter of many years . . . from the exercise of that quality wherein they were bred . . . lingered under the heavy yoke of poverty, and fed themselves and family with hunger, sighs and tears'.

60

CHAPTER FIVE

The Restoration Theatre

The only plays that Cromwell had permitted were those acted in schools. Authority, however, was not always alert and even, on occasion, turned a blind eye. The actors crept back; first privately, in the houses of the nobility, and then, tentatively and sporadically, in the inn-yards. That the populace's love of the theatre was only dormant is evidenced by the great flood of plays that poured from the printing presses during the eighteen years of the interregnum, and the not infrequent occasions when players and public alike risked severe state fines for joining in clandestine performances. There grew up a substantial body of opinion that pressed for the reopening of the theatres, employing such worthy arguments as 'Some 'scape a sermon, whom a play might win'.

The highly skilled and beautiful boys have grown up and 'grown out of use, like cracked organ-pipes, and have faces as old as our flags' in the eighteen years during which the theatres have been closed. In May of 1656, a 'pleasant, jolly woman' (who later admitted to Pepys that she had been unable to learn her part and couldn't remember the music) stood in the wings waiting for her cue. 'This is Ianthe, the Sicilian flower'—and on she tripped, Mrs Coleman, the first professional actress to appear on the English stage (and Cromwell still alive). There are other claimants to the honour, notably an unnamed actress who played Desdemona, but what is important is not who was first but that, at about this time, it became customary for women to appear on the public stage in the female roles hitherto always acted by the boy-players. Mrs Coleman adorned the first of the regular performances that Davenant had been permitted to give in the miniature theatre he had erected in his private—but stately—house, his own *The Siege of Rhodes*, the first English opera.

Cromwell's death, in 1658, and the unpopularity of his son as a successor saw the end of Puritan domination. The actors had already chanced surreptitious performances

61

Oliver Cromwell, from a painting after Samuel Cooper in the mid-1650s. (*Copyright National Portrait Gallery*)

at the Old Elizabethan theatres, with little or no scenery, by the time that General Monk marched into London at the head of the Royalist forces. Within two months of King Charles's return, in May of 1660, matters were regularized by a royal warrant which gave Davenant and Killigrew a virtual monopoly of the stage. Before the year was out, their two companies were competing for the London audience. Within a year Davenant had reconstructed the Tennis Court in Lincoln's Inn Fields as a new theatre; and within three years Killigrew had built his new Theatre in Drury Lane at a cost of £2,400.

The actors were fortunate in the interest that the King took in theatre matters. This was in no way limited to the considerable number of Command Performances at Court (it took the actors eight or nine years to get the money for these) or to the more intimate services rendered to her much-loving King by Nell Gwynne (she got paid rather more promptly). Charles took delight in attending personally at the public theatres; he inter-

Interior of a Restoration theatre

Some idea of the appearance of the proscenium arch and side-boxes of the Duke's Theatre is illustrated by this engraving published in the 1673 edition of Settle's play *The Empress of Morocco*. (*Copyright British Museum*)

vened as referee in many of the disputes that arose among actors; he even lent the players the royal coronation suits. Both companies suffered from the fact that there were really only enough theatre-goers to support one company. It was not only the Puritans who stayed away. Most of the middle class and 'many of the more Civilized Part of the Town . . . shun the Theatre as they would a House of Scandal'. The players made no effort to encourage the general citizenry but concentrated upon making their performances attractive to the small Court audience. The theatre became (in Allardyce Nicoll's* graphic phrase) a 'toy of the upper classes'.

Killigrew proved a bad manager at the King's house, and there was constant wrangling among his unhappy players. Davenant had the better actors (Betterton in particular) and his scenic innovations excited great curiosity. But success for either company was only intermittent. 'Mighty empty', says Pepys on going to the theatre and he commonly found one theatre empty when the other was offering a new piece. Even quite successful plays ran for no more than three performances and many new plays were seen for only one performance. A new play was always more likely to bring a full house than was a revival, and one with elaborate new scenery was even more likely to succeed. The rival houses found themselves in the financially dangerous position of trying to outbid each other for popular favour by spending more and more on scenery.

In 1671 the Davenant-Betterton company spent as much as £9,000 on a new theatre,

The Restoration Theatre

* Professor Nicoll is our major contemporary theatre historian, covering the period from the Restoration to the end of the nineteenth century in five volumes of immaculate research.

Spectacular scenery used in the Duke's Theatre is illustrated by these four scenes from Settle's *The Empress of Morocco*. (*Copyright British Museum*)

the Duke's in Dorset Gardens. The joint attractions of the great Betterton's acting, the much admired beauties of the new theatre and increasingly spectacular scenery put the Duke's men well ahead of their declining rivals. Jolly, a third rival, after much conflict had been bought off by being given charge of a joint 'nursery' for both theatres where young performers were trained. Indignant protests from inhabitants in the neighbourhood drew from the King a message 'that Playhouses should be pulled down when the Meeting houses (places of worship) were'.

Fire wrecked the Theatre Royal, Drury Lane, in 1672, leaving the King's actors (as the Killigrew company were named) in such a sorry plight that they appealed to the King for funds. He sent them a letter for presentation to parish churches soliciting contributions. Many parishes complied!

The new Drury Lane theatre opened in 1674. Poor attendance, the burden of accumulated debt, and the incompetence of Killigrew's son as manager (which so riled the actors that they refused to appear) led the King two years later to intervene and grant the actors the right to govern themselves. Soon they found themselves unable to muster large enough audiences to continue playing. Finally, in 1682, the rival companies were united with Betterton at their head and continued thus for twelve years. Success attended this arrangement in its early years. Later it became apparent that even one theatre might have its difficulties in finding a sufficient audience, a sad comparison with conditions some thirty or forty years previously when a smaller population had supported as many as six theatres.

The Restoration Comedy of Manners Immoral, licentious, vulgar, brutal, immodest, indelicate, vicious, sensual, evil, crude, carnal, corrupt, degenerate, for moral perverts, pornographic, filth. A bare three or four pages from a major present-day history of the theatre yields this heady catalogue. The mid-Victorian Macaulay is even more uncomfortable: 'too filthy to handle and too noisome even to approach'. The anxiety to bring no blush to any maiden cheek is so great that, even in books of our own times, we still meet with great smoke-clouds of evasion when it comes to simply giving a name to what the plays are about. *L'amour* they say, finding a kind of safety in relegating the subject to the Continent—where such matters so sadly prevail. And we have all, moralists and immoralists alike, had to filch from the French the one phrase in comfortable common use—'having an *affaire* with someone'. One sees one of the difficulties; there is no word in everyday English for the sexual act that is not a swear-word.

Nowadays most of the fig-leaves are off; we can get down to bed-rock and call a jade a jade. What is (charmingly) called The Comedy of Manners portrays a society that exalted above all other pursuits the pleasures of sex and romance between people not married to each other. The successfully promiscuous man was regarded not as a sinner but as the admired example of the age. Marriage was regarded not as a secure state of grace but as a riotously fit subject for mockery. A state of hedonism was declared fashionable and society became one great 'pleasure' garden. In the long battle between the biological urge and the social urge, between our desire for liberty and our desire for security, this particular skirmish left the cavalier gallant and his most willing female partners in joy a freedom to rove never enjoyed since. The foray into these uncharted waters over, man took cover,

**Don Juan left holding
the baby**

Don John, 'a curious night-walker' out roving for beauties, passes by the house of the
most famed (and best guarded) of them all. A door opens, an old woman thrusts a bundle
into his arms . . . and is gone. He who has 'known wenches this long, all the ways of
wenches, their snares and subtleties' is left, holding the baby, without even a sight of the
beauty. The engraving shows David Garrick as Don John in Beaumont and Fletcher's
The Chances. (*Author's collection*)

scuttling back into the harbour of matrimony; from whence he has ever since alternated between making moral stump-speeches from the quay-side and putting out to sea under cover of dark for the odd act of piracy. The problem is shelved, not solved; we embrace an illusion rather than face up to an uncomfortable reality. But, for this brief space of time, English society made its most notable experiment in the relationship between the sexes. It attempted to find a working (a very hard-working) compromise between the liberty of dalliance and the security of matrimony. It found the two to be incompatible. Its dramatists found the experiment and its results to be comic. They wrote some of the best comedies in the language—and some of the worst. Disgust with the latter need no longer rob us of pleasure in the former.

'I could never connect these sports of a witty fancy in any shape with any result to be drawn from them to imitation in real life. . . . They have got out of Christendom into the land of—what shall I call it?—of cuckoldry—the Utopia of gallantry, where pleasure is duty, and the manners perfect freedom. It is altogether a speculative scene of things, which has no reference to the world that is.' So says Charles Lamb. 'Perhaps he thought that he could even play his readers a child's trick, and persuade them that Congreve's fine ladies and gentlemen were doing nothing but "making as if". Most assuredly he was mistaken.' So says Leigh Hunt; and there is little doubt that he was right. If all things done in the comedies were not actually done in life, they could have been; and other equally 'Utopian' things were certainly done. It is the very perfection of the artificial style in the writing that leads us to suppose the gallant's actions to be equally artificial. But we may be sure that these things were; and that society found a way of enjoying them. (Until the children of their pleasure grew up.)

The Restoration Theatre

For the tedious remaining few who would ban the plays on moral grounds—and for the undecided—a paragraph of protest is necessary. One child out of every eight born in London during the last recorded year was born a bastard; by the time they come to marry, more young people of today have lost their virginity than have kept it; and priests enter into admirably relaxed discussion before the huge television audience of these and the many other manifestations that our society is not accepting matrimony as the only playground for the sexes. We may or may not deplore the state of affairs but we shall gain nothing by pretending that it does not exist. There is no virtue in beating about a bush until all its leaves are off, its trunk mutilated and its roots starved. After nearly 300 years, our own society is closer to Charles's fashion in love than it has been at any time in the intervening years. We may surely take pleasure (and even some profit) in seeking what the more engaging of Charles's dramatists have to tell us. Their impertinent stories are pertinent.

The characters in the Comedy of Manners are stock characters and their stories vary little. The Airy Gallant may have many names (Loveless, Wildair, Horner, Sir Positive At-All) but only one character—'a great defier of all ladies in the way of marriage, otherwise their much loose servant'. The ladies are either 'witty followers of the chase' like Mrs Love-it or Lady Lurewell; country cousins bent on metropolitan mischief; or dainty sugar-cake angels (Fidelia, Angelica). Essential subsidiary characters are the Cuckolded Husband and a foolish Fop or two to divert by aping the Gallants (Lord

Foppington, Sparkish, Sir Novelty Fashion). Just as their names leave us in little doubt as to their characters, so does the title of one play—*The Wive's Excuse or Cuckolds Make Themselves*—leave us in little suspense as to the story of them all. The scope of the action is so limited that whole stretches of any one play become little more than repetitions of similar stretches in other plays. If all the plots of all the innumerable Restoration comedies of manners were welded into one (no very difficult matter) there is substance enough for only one play's plot. This limitation is imposed, primarily, by two main considerations: the limitations of the Gallant himself as major protagonist; and the still further narrowing of his capabilities when he is confined within the wrong convention of the comedy of manners.

The Gallant For some one hundred and fifty years this one character of the Gallant plays one of the major roles in the comedies of the times—and for an appreciable part of that time he occupies the very centre of the stage. 'Whistle and she'll come to you' says one of the early gallants (written by Fletcher in Jacobean times—*Wit Without Money*, *c*. 1614). From then on, the Gallant edges his way ever nearer to the stage's centre. Under the first Charles, with Shirley the major dramatist in the latter part of the reign, he is well on the way to establishing his supremacy. With the return of the second Charles and the Cavaliers triumphant, he is undisputed master, routing Roundhead cuckolds on a stage dominated by the comedy of manners. The coming of the comedy of sentiment in the early eighteenth century blunts his vitality and severely threatens his supremacy, but he is not finally put in his place until the coming of Goldsmith and Sheridan in the 1770s.

The best of the written gallants have an abounding vitality, wit and guile—and every man must give to them one vulgar fraction of his envy. But, for all his charm, society has found the gallant to be a deprived (and depriving) creature. He gives all he has—but has not enough to give. A prodigal spendthrift, with more false counters than coins in his purse, he takes more than he can pay for. The heart of the matter is that the Gallant is as much the cause of pathos as of pleasure. When his story is placed in its proper context—tragi-comedy—he gains this extra dimension and his story gains a whole new freedom of movement. Exposed at the centre of a comedy of manners, his potential is found to be so limited (he who boasts so often of his powers) that he slightens it; and is in turn slightened by it, for his wit and industry pall when unduly extended; and this they must be when denied the greater range of action that pathos permits in tragi-comedy.

The sense of proportion that Shakespeare brings to his handling of the Gallant magnificently demonstrates one facet of his supremacy. Dalliance is a planet not a sun and Lucio in *Measure for Measure* is superbly in perspective as he glints brightly on the periphery of that play's sterner action. Witty and charming, Lucio (the Cavalier) can spend generously because he cares little. Chaste but chilling, Isabella (the Puritan) must hoard prudently because she cares too much. They stand at opposite extremes, poles apart, and Lucio's attempts to reach across the intervening arena have all the wry pathos of a firework attempting to advise a statue. When they enter the arena they are punished, as they must be; he for his inability to care more for the good name of others; she for her inability to care less for her own good name. Those who give uncaringly and those who hoard ungivingly can only inhabit the periphery of life's more temperate give-and-take. The Cavalier and the Puritan, life drawn to extremes, are both given Measure for Measure, their just and proper place in the play's society.

There is not so very much more to be said about the Gallant than Shakespeare says about Lucio. When the Cavaliers glamourise him into the centre of their comedies, he narrows down the whole horizon of the drama into a peep-show. 'What the Butler Saw' is not enough of life to see; and the minor dramatists of the time give us little more than this.

The Major Dramatists The miracle is that the major dramatists, working within such severe limitations (a fashion more rigid than any censor), should have given us some unforgettable masterpieces. What they write about is only a fraction of man's interests and their characters are an even smaller fraction of man's society. But what we can see as only one corner of life, they saw as a whole world; and the light they threw onto it is so dazzling that we are made rich by their work out of all proportion to its worthiness. Though they forsook verse for prose, though they elevated wit far above life, it is, surprisingly, as poets that they claim our best remembrance. They should be read for the poise and precision of their language as much as for their fun. The writers move like fencers, not fighters. The slight and polished foils flash and glint and victory is all a matter of grace in the scoring of points. Blood has no place on swords like these, nor can death or wounding, defeat or rescue have any part in a contest whose only prize is the game itself. When all is done, the heart has beat but little faster and not even the fighters are breathless. Life remains untouched. But we have known an enchantment.

All husbands and wives spend some part of their time measuring their partners against an imagined ideal and their partnership against an imagined perfection. (It is not only adolescents who are hero-worshippers.) Some gain by the process, some lose; but it is only those who have abandoned a proper part of hope, and yielded to the improper quiet that despair can bring, who refrain from chasing the romantic will-o'-the-wisps. The Restoration writers' gallants and rakish ladies personify one part of all our longings. Which man among us would not willingly surrender to a day in which we matched ourselves against Congreve's Millimant or encountered the less conscious temptations of Wycherley's Margery Pinchwife? Which free woman could shut the door on Farquhar's Sir Harry Wildair? A lifetime of any of them would be insufferably tedious; but any life could count time spent with them amongst its properest devotions to gaiety.

Congreve 'The four principal writers of this style of comedy (which I think the best) are undoubtedly Wycherley, Congreve, Vanbrugh and Farquhar' says Hazlitt, and posterity has confirmed his judgement. Congreve is commonly regarded as the best of the four and his *The Way of the World* as the supreme masterpiece of its kind, 'the final and flawless evidence of his incomparable powers . . . the crowning work of his genius—the unequalled and unapproached masterpiece of English comedy'. Swinburne is not the only man of letters whose praise has erred on the side of extravagance and it is with something of relief that one encounters Graham Greene's present-day judgement: 'Congreve, like a smooth schoolboy, stole all the prizes.' What Congreve could do, in the matter of writing a comedy,

(1) William Congreve—Kneller's portrait of 1709, engraved by
Faber, 1733. (*Copyright National Portrait Gallery*)

he did better than anybody; what he could not do (and there was much), he did worse
than even minor writers. *The Way of the World* is unequalled (though it is not unapproached) for the wit and elegance of its speech. It is all of a delight for dons; but, on
the stage, it is something of a dog's dinner. We are presented with the paradoxical picture
of the most sublimely coherent speakers in our comic drama tangling and stumbling
through a blithely incoherent action. There is nothing ruder in the whole of Restoration
comedy than the perfunctory way the dramatist bungles his characters on and off the
stage; and the ramshackle denouement is an affront to his virtues and our patience.

Even in the library we have a right to expect that a play (particularly an artificial
comedy of manners) should be something more than an anthology of well-shaped speeches.
Congreve's passion for shapeliness often takes him no further than the length of an anti-
thesis. Moral latitude is not the enemy here, but dramatic longitude. The further the play
goes, the less shapely it becomes, and, as sentence follows each fine sentence, a kind of
progressive deterioration sets in. Few pages are shaped as well as each speech in them,
few scenes as well as each page; fewer acts as well as each scene; and no play as well as
any part of it. Sentence is laid next to sentence something in the manner of a road-maker
placing his stones unendingly end to end. But a play's construction is more that of a
building than a road; and any residence that is to be desirable must be something more
than a jumbling together of rooms, just as each room must be something more than a
mere attachment of wall to wall. We are entitled to expect of an architect that he give a
becoming and proper shape to the whole edifice. A perfect comedy of manners in the Congreve style should have an architecture as strictly formal as that of a sonnet. It should

cohere. *The Way of the World* should be read for all the undeniable delight there is in it; studied for its utmost refinements in literary style; and shunned like the plague for its lumpen laziness in dramatic construction.

How one wishes that collaboration had been the order of Congreve's day—for any one of his three colleagues could have fashioned his play for him. As it was, the play failed at its first performance and has teased its players ever since. Congreve himself wrote better-made plays; *Love for Love* is far superior in the matter of construction. But, though that has many fine things, it has no one character as memorable as Millimant nor any one scene as transcendent as that which she shares with Mirabell. Millimant is, in Hazlitt's words, 'the ideal heroine of the comedy of high life . . . to whom pleasure is as familiar as the air she draws; elegance worn as a part of her dress; wit, the habitual language which she hears and speaks; love, a matter of course.' When Mirabell tells her 'You are no longer handsome when you've lost your lover; your beauty dies upon the instant; for beauty is the lover's gift', she retorts 'O the vanity of these men! . . . Beauty the lover's gift! Lord! What is a lover, that it can give? Why, one makes lovers as fast as one pleases, and they live as long as one pleases, and they die as soon as one pleases; and then, if one pleases, one makes more.' In exquisite raillery, they examine the possibilities of marriage. 'My dear liberty, shall I leave thee? My faithful solitude, my darling contemplation, must I bid you then adieu? Ay-h, adieu. My morning thoughts, agreeable wakings, indolent slumbers . . . I can't do't, 'tis more than impossible—positively, Mirabell, I'll lie abed in a morning as long as I please.' And when Mirabell says that he'll get up in the morning as early as he pleases: 'Ah! Idle creature. . . .' Finally, after submitting to him the most enchantingly impossible list of provisos, she supposes that she 'may, by degrees, dwindle into a wife'. While Millimant is on the stage, it seems churlish to deny Congreve supremacy. But no sooner have we been wooed and won by the 'witching creature than she's whisked from our sight. We'd give our whole purse for another prolonged view of her but she's never again exposed at length—Congreve, like some short-sighted covetous old bawd, fobs us off with his drab penny-ordinaries.

Congreve is something less successful with Mirabell and his other gallants. He doesn't love them as he does Millimant—and they are not as lovable. There is a touch of fatigue about them; they lack the abundance of vitality that captivates one in Farquhar's heroes. The ideal gallant should be lusty and vital as well as witty. In Congreve these qualities are never quite in balance and when his gallants flaunt their nether virtues they seem to disrupt the writer's elaborate and brittle filigree-work.

Farquhar is the master in this field. What a match for Millimant would have been his Sir Harry Wildair, 'a gentleman of most happy circumstances, born to a plentiful estate, has had a genteel and easy education, free from the rigidness of teachers and pedantry of schools. His florid constitution, being never ruffled by misfortune, nor stinted in its pleasures, has rendered him entertaining to others, and easy to himself: turning all passion into gaiety of humour'. There is an exquisite balance between Sir Harry and his foil in *The Constant Couple*—Colonel Standard, a disbanded soldier of entrancing probity. The good soldier attempts to disturb Sir Harry's equanimity—'But suppose you had lost a

(2) George Farquhar. (*Copyright Mander and Mitchenson Theatre Collection*)

mistress?' only to be met with the bland—'Why, then would I get another.' Standard persists—'But suppose you were discarded by the woman you love, that would surely trouble you?' Little does the huff-bluff Colonel know his man—'You're mistaken, Colonel; my love is neither romantically honourable, nor meanly mercenary. 'Tis only a pitch of gratitude: while she loves me, I love her; when she desists, the obligation's void.'

Sir Harry is tricked into thinking Angelica's virtuous home a bawdy-house; and the comedy of their scenes together depends on his bursting impatience to be settling accounts with the puzzled but enchanted girl of sixteen. These scenes, written with great liveliness and a disarming good nature, are the most memorable in the play. It is interesting to compare them with Congreve's great scene. In this, there is no reason why either Millimant or Mirabell should leave their seats; they are much of a mind and share a conversation. Farquhar's people on the other hand, share a confrontation of opposites, and Sir Harry buzzes round Angelica like an eager gadfly. Farquhar is all for the doing, which he enlivens with an abundant elegance of good humour; Congreve is all for the telling, which he illuminates with an infinite elegance of wit.

Is it too much to say that the comparison is between a delicate etching in monochrome and a bustling picture replete with colour? Perhaps. But Farquhar's is certainly the broader canvas. In their pictures of the little London social world, where Congreve decries poverty of wit, Farquhar decries poverty—stark poverty. ' 'Tis still my maxim, that there is no scandal like rags, nor any crime so shameful as poverty.' (Here, and elsewhere, he reaches across two centuries and joins hands with Bernard Shaw.) His good natured creatures rattle past at such a rate, and are so agreeable, that we are in constant danger of missing the sting in the tail of many of their pleasantries.

Just as his social awareness makes Farquhar see more of London than does Congreve, so do his ranging sympathies make him see more of England than London; he is at home, where Congreve would be lost—at loose with country folk in the country places where his two later plays, *The Recruiting Officer* and *The Beaux' Stratagem*, takes place.

Farquhar came latest in time of the four dramatists under consideration, when Fop's Walks and London drawing-rooms had long been the only scenes. Audiences, grown weary of the milieu, must have been ripe for a change. What a welcome they get from the jovial country inn-keeper when the curtain rises on *The Beaux' Stratagem*—and what a holiday welcome they must have given to Farquhar's warming country folk. Boniface, who has now in his cellar 'ten tun of the best ale in Staffordshire; 'tis smooth as oil, sweet as milk, clear as amber, and strong as brandy; and will be just fourteen year old the fifth day of next March, old style. . . . I have fed purely upon ale. I have eat my ale, drank my ale, and I always sleep upon ale.' His daughter, Cherry 'What a rogue is my father! My father? I deny it. My mother was a good, generous, free-hearted woman, and I can't tell how far her good nature might have extended for the good of her children.' This is no tedious bumpkin, no cliché character from the theatre's stock-in-trade, for Farquhar knew his country people at first hand. When the town gentleman thinks to ruffle Cherry with a blunt approach 'Prithee, instruct me, I would fain make love to you, but I don't know what to say'—he is very promptly outwitted. 'Why, did you never make love to anybody before?' Farquhar delighted in pricking the bubble of pretentiousness. Gibbet, the highwayman, due to be hanged if caught thieving, when told 'Come, rogue, if you have a short prayer, say it' answers 'Sir, I have no prayer at all; the government has provided a chaplain to say prayers for us on these occasions.' This sort of jesting courage Farquhar knew, too well, at first hand. The play was written in six weeks as he lay, in dire poverty, on his death-bed with 'a settled sickness on him'. He was twenty-nine.

Vanbrugh is something more workaday than his colleagues. Where Congreve is driven on to write by the pursuit of style, and Farquhar is guided by a nice awareness of human nature and driven by want of bread, Vanbrugh has no higher pretensions than to divert his fellow gentlemen. Bonamy Dobree* has his measure perfectly—'he took life as he found it, and left it there'. But, if he used the theatre as a toy, he at least troubled to learn its tricks. His plays are well made. And if he sought to do little more than to jot down what he heard, he had a good ear—particularly for the domestic scene, and for the 'wrong notes' of cant or hypocrisy. When Lady Arabella in *A Journey to London* is asked 'If you won't hear of your faults, how is it likely you would ever mend them?' She replies 'Why, I don't intend to mend 'em. I can't mend 'em, I have told you so a hundred times; you know I have tried to do it, over and over, and it hurts me so, I can't bear it. Why, don't you know, my Lord, that whenever (just to please you only) I have gone about to wean myself from a fault (one of my faults, I mean, that I love dearly) hasn't it put me so out of humour, you would scarce endure the house with me. . . . Weaning? . . . Don't you see your true religious people, when they go about to wean themselves, and have solemn days of fasting and praying, on purpose to help them, does it not so disorder them, there's no

* Professor Dobree's *Restoration Comedy* has much more to say than many longer books.

(3) Sir John Vanbrugh, from a painting attributed to Thomas Murray, *c.* 1718. (*Copyright National Portrait Gallery*)

coming near 'em; are they not as cross as the devil? And then they don't do the business neither; for next day their faults are just where they were the day before.' This scene, and some few like it, are the exceptions that prove the rule that 'He is no writer at all, as to mere authorship'. But Hazlitt goes on to add 'but he makes up for it by a prodigious fund of comic invention . . . in dramatic contrast and unlooked-for situations, where the different parties play upon one another's failings, and into one another's hands, keeping up the jest like a game of battledore and shuttlecock.' His plays act better than they read, though, even in print, their zest and gusto is always apparent. *The Relapse* is the finest of the finished plays (the unfinished fragment, *A Journey to London*, has his finest writing). Lord Foppington is one of the funniest of the many Fops that throng the plays and Miss Hoyden only a little short of supremacy among the country girls. 'It's well they've got me a husband, or ecod, I'd marry the baker' she says; and when mischievous visitors are announced, out rings the order 'Let loose the greyhound, and lock up Hoyden.' If Vanbrugh is the least of the four dramatists, at his best he is very good company.

Wycherley came first in time but has been left until last for reasons not entirely perverse. More than any of his colleagues, he was at the core (if not the heart) of his times and the comedy of manners. Congreve makes of his satire a thing of fantasy, light as air; Farquhar lends it an air of romance; Vanbrugh's rough-and-tumble borders on farce. There is the savagery of resentment about Wycherley. Congreve was a gentleman and a

74

scholar, Vanbrugh a knight, and they wrote from inside a society that accepted them. Farquhar and Wycherley wrote from outside a society that rejected them. Farquhar was a soldier of fortune and too full of nature and good spirits to be resentful. Wycherley was uncertain, bitter and violent.

In Wycherley there lived two men, the Puritan and the Cavalier; and, surely, there was a third of him, watching them both. He is always at war with himself, punching away at his own head—with his third man the uneasiest of referees (for the rule-book has been mislaid). The extremes to which his dual nature pushed him make his life read like a Gothic novel, full of haunting incredibilities. We may presume that the Cavalier was dominant when as a young man he wrote two plays by the time he was twenty-one. Was it the Puritan in him that kept them secret and held from performance till ten years later? Or was it a talent for introspective self-examination that led him to doubt their readiness? Whatever it was, the first two plays are evidence of a mind far from decided as to its intentions. In some scenes, he seems to find the follies of the times cause for no more than laughter and has no other concern than to present them as diverting; in other scenes, the same follies bring forth so virulent a satirical castigation that he seems bent on scourging himself quite as vengefully as his society. The conventions in which he writes veer from elegant high comedy to the most savage and brutal satire; and then, with barely a breath between, on to the most insipid romantic sentiment. His third play, *The Plain Dealer*, was written when he was twenty-five and not performed until he refashioned it ten years later. It adds to the impression that here is a man who cannot decide whether he respects or loathes himself and seeks an uneasy catharsis by spending his furies on those elements in the society around him that reflect his own inner turmoil. In only one play—and it is his masterpiece—does he succeed in bringing his conflicting talents into a proper focus. In *The Country Wife* he seems at last sure of what he means to do—and does it superbly. You may take it, if you will, at its face value; and, provided you are not too cluttered with moral encumbrances, laughter will have it's way with you. But Wycherley's one great stroke of comic invention, on which the whole play turns, is also the source of its most savage irony. Yet this irony is held under such strict control that it never obtrudes on the simple enjoyment of the play's action but hangs in the mind and echoes there, adding further and deeper pleasures as one ruminates in afterthought.

The Restoration's rakish ladies did not care what mischief they were up to, so long as their good name—their 'honour' as they called it—remained untouched. Neither anxious husbands in their homes nor the censorious world outside were likely to trouble their heads if the ladies entertained effeminate fops over the teacups. Where there was no threat, there was no danger—and no demur. Horner, Wycherley's gallant in the play, hits on the brilliant device of persuading a doctor to report him (falsely) throughout the town as impotent. Husbands scurry to thrust him on their wives. 'If I can but abuse the husbands, I'll soon disabuse the wives.' He is soon at loose with them over the teacups and it is not long after that Lady Fidget is able to report that he has had her 'toiling and moiling for the prettiest piece of china' in the next room. Poised against the free-roving young Horner is a 'reformed' rake of forty-nine, Pinchwife. Once 'one that knew the town so much, and women so well' he has, with 'grave circumspection', married a country wife. Under

(4) William Wycherley, from a copy of Lely's portrait, *c.* 1668. (*Copyright National Portrait Gallery*)

the happy delusion that 'he that marries is a fool; but he's a greater that does not marry a fool' he thinks to keep her to himself by proclaiming her as ugly, ill-bred, silly and innocent. Margery Pinchwife, the country girl, has her own reasons for coming to town and we are soon made aware that the blood races as fast for the simple as for the sophisticated. Her husband, a growing slave to jealousy, forces her to dress as a man, thinking, with ironic *naïveté*, thus to keep her safe from Horner's growing interest. Few things in the play are better than the comedy Wycherley achieves by contrasting Margery's simple blunt candour with the elegant artificialities of the town ladies. But they all go the same way. The play ends with a cuckold's dance.

You need, perhaps, to be something of a Cavalier to enjoy the play without finding it, as one modern critic does, 'the acme of impropriety'. And you need, perhaps, to have something of the Puritan in you to catch its ironic echoes and set yourself questioning in how many senses the play's 'virile' society is truly impotent, in how many senses Horner himself is impotent (is he not doomed to become Pinchwife when he is his age?), how very sophisticated is the simple girl, and how very simple, even primitive, are the sophisticated ladies. It has to be said that the play is blunt and brutal; Wycherley seldom plays at hoodman's blind. A whore is a whore and 'the pox' is something more than a routine swear-word. If you have not read the plays of the period before and are inquisitive, take Farquhar for your first companion, progress to Congreve and leave Wycherley till the last.

One sees Congreve standing don-wise and hesitant at the door of the house, torn between his notes and warmer notions. Vanbrugh comes stumbling roly-poly down the stairs, misses his footing and thumps to the ground, cursing happily. Farquhar walks in careless, takes his pleasure, agreeably passes the time of day, and is on his graceful way out, when Wycherley comes down bluntly thrusting past, one arm raised as if to conceal his presence there, the other striking out blindly, savagely condemning self and all, and dashes, spent but tormented, from the loathed loves where he has cut off his poor 'pocked nose to spite his once handsome face. Wycherley has earned the last word. There is as much of life (and more of a disturbed, feeling heart) in his brutalities as there is in the romance and elegance of the others. If you have the stomach for it.

Restoration Drama Though, in retrospect, it is the Comedy of Manners that appears to dominate and typify the period, there were many rival claims to the attentions of the playgoers of the time. At the beginning of the period the theatres, of necessity, concerned themselves primarily with revivals of the pre-Commonwealth plays, with Beaumont and Fletcher still proving more popular than Shakespeare. The manners school saw its dawn in Etheredge; Jonson's 'humours' school saw a rather dirty dusk in Shadwell. Mrs Aphra Behn was the first woman to earn her living by writing and her comedies of intrigue fully merit the recognition given them by her male contemporaries, even if they do not belong to the first class.

Dryden ventures into the Comedy of Manners with his *Marriage à la Mode*, only a little short of the best in this kind; and some others nearly as low as the worst. He also

(5) John Dryden, from a copy of Kneller's portrait, 1698. (*Copyright National Portrait Gallery*)

The great Restoration actor—Betterton

A contemporary engraving by van der Gucht of Kneller's painting (1710). (*Author's collection*)

Betterton as Hamlet

The engraved frontispiece to *Hamlet* in Rowe's Shakespeare, 1709, is thought by some to represent Betterton in the part and to give some indication of design, costume and stage business of the time. Note the 'down-gyv'd' stocking, and the overturned chair. (*Copyright British Museum*)

made a considerable contribution to what is known as the 'Love and Honour' school of Heroic tragedy, so called because it was between these two characteristics that the hero was forced to choose in a series of violent actions. Written in flamboyant rhyme, there was too much of declamation and rant in them to permit of any very enduring life in the theatre. Dryden's major tragedy, *All for Love*, shares its subject with Shakespeare's *Antony and Cleopatra* and, if the latter had never been written, might well hold an honoured place on the stage to this day. It is long overdue for revival; but one can sympathize with the manager who funks it, knowing that inevitably the critics will inform him (and the public) that 'it's not as good as the other'. Yet few plays have so strong a claim to be considered the best tragedy in verse after those of Shakespeare. Its major rival is Otway's *Venice Preserv'd*, which has seen more performances over the years than any non-Shakespearean tragedy. With this and his other major tragedy, *The Orphan*, Otway stands high above the not very tempting serious theatre of his times, most of which is much too solemn and declamatory for present-day tastes.

Restoration Players Betterton. 'How Shakespeare wrote, all men who have a taste for nature may read and know—but with what higher rapture would he still be read could they conceive how Betterton play'd him. . . . I never heard a line in tragedy come from Betterton wherein my judgement, my ear and my imagination were not fully satisfied.' So says Colley Cibber in his memoirs. That Betterton was not betrayed into the 'Grand Manner' by the fustian in the many contemporary plays in which he appeared is made quite clear by another excerpt: 'Betterton never wanted fire or force when his character demanded it; yet where it was not demanded, he never prostituted his power to the low ambition of a false applause. . . . I have heard him say, he never thought any kind of it (applause) equal to an attentive silence.' His behaviour off-stage appears to have been as proper as it was on-stage. He stood head and shoulders above the players of his time and was a good model and teacher to his successors.

Nell Gwynne's romantic rise from orange-girl (as the euphemism goes) to King's mistress is legendary. She appears to have given abundant satisfaction as an actress, too. Deficient in tragedy, she triumphed in comedy and the speaking of prologues and epilogues. She triumphed, in fact, wherever her abundant natural vitality and charms could be displayed, and she achieved great popularity. She was a warm, generous-hearted creature and the cause of much gaiety—qualities not always shared by other equally easy-virtued actresses and female courtiers of her time. Her contemporaries, Mrs Barry and Mrs Bracegirdle, apart from their excellence in their profession, shared the common predilection of the times for an even older profession. The temptation to elaborate on their astonishing powers in either field had better give way to Cibber's magnificent description of Mrs Mountford. It brings before us the whole atmosphere of a performance of the times. 'Melantha (in Dryden's *Marriage à la Mode*) is as finish'd an Impertinent as ever flutter'd in a Drawing-Room, and seems to contain the most compleat System of Female Foppery that could possibly be crowded into the tortured Form of a Fine Lady. Her Language, Dress, Motion, Manners, Soul, and Body, are in a continual Hurry to be something more than is necessary or commendable. . . . A Gallant never seen before, delivers her a Letter

Nell Gwynne, from a painting in the studio of Lely, *c.* 1675. (*Copyright National Portrait Gallery*)

from her Father recommending him to her good Graces as an honourable Lover. Here now, one would think, she might naturally shew a little of the Sexe's decent Reserve, tho' never so slightly cover'd! No, Sir; not a Tittle of it; Modesty is the Virtue of a poor-soul'd Country Gentlewoman; she is too much a Court Lady to be under so vulgar a Confusion; she reads the Letter, therefore, with a careless dropping Lip and an erected Brow, humming it hastily over as if she were impatient to outgo her Father's Commands by making a compleat Conquest of him at once; and that the Letter might not embarrass her Attack, crack! she crumbles it at once into her Palm and pours upon him her whole Artillery of Airs, Eyes and Motion; down goes her dainty, diving Body to the Ground, as if she were sinking under the conscious Load of her own Attractions; then launches into a flood of fine Language and Compliment, still playing her Chest forward in fifty Falls and Risings, like a Swan upon waving Water; and, to complete her Impertinence, she is so rapidly fond of her own Wit that she will not give her Lover Leave to praise it; Silent assenting Bows and vain Endeavours to speak are all the share of the Conversation he is admitted to, which at last he is relieved from by her Engagement to half a Score Visits, which she *swims* from him to make, with a Promise to return in a Twinkling.'

Conclusion On Charles's death, in 1685, James II acceded to the throne. In his short reign, performances were given at court and, on occasion, the King went to the public playhouse. William and Mary, who came to rule four years later, showed a lesser pre-occupation with the theatre than their predecessors. The character of audiences was slowly changing. Many of the gallants were away at the wars and the players began to turn an eye to the citizenry. 'Some squeamish females of renown' found their way to the theatres and began to exercise a chastening influence. The Comedies of Manners with their frank and free stories of philandering had delighted Charles's court; but now the new upper-middle class sought to impose a sense of decorum on the theatre. The changing mood of the times was reflected in uncertain policy, poor attendance and decorous but dull plays. A petition of Betterton's paints an unhappy picture: 'It appears by the receipts and constant Charges of the Theatres for some years past, that the Town will not maintain two Playhouses. That the two Company's have by their bidding against each other for Singers, Dancers &c who are generally Strangers, rais'd the prices so high that both are impoverisht by it, and most of their Proffits carry'd away by Forreigners. That both Companys have been forc'd for their Subsistance to bring on the Stage, Dancers on the Ropes, Tumblers, Vaulters, Ladders dancers &c and thereby debas'd the Theatre and almost levell'd it with Bartholomew ffaire.'

Interim Summary The British Drama came of age with the Elizabethans, sowed some very wild oats during the Restoration, then, with the coming of the eighteenth century entered a long period of ill-health. It is a pertinent moment for an interim diagnosis.

'The Elizabethan age was an age of discovery, in which every Tom, Dick and Harry could feel he had a share. But the greatest discovery of all was of the boundless range of the human mind and spirit, and of the marvels that lay within the compass of their most potent instrument, the word. We can hardly conceive how it felt to learn, within so short a space of time, what English words could be made to do. We bathed in words, and splashed each other with them, like children on their first morning at the seaside. Words became an intoxicant. . . . They blew in a great gale. . . . And in this discovery too the plain man could share . . . for it was in the words that players spoke that the English Renaissance found its culminating expression.' Mr Bridges-Adams's* words admirably catch the wonder of the dawn and the hey-day. The poets explored Man's whole estate. When the Elizabethans had done with the living-room, it seemed that there was little more to be said. Only the abnormal was left, the nooks and crannies and the secret places. James took them down into the cellar; and when they came up for air, Charles whisked them off to the bedroom.

* His book *The Irresistible Theatre* is not only infectiously attractive but valuable because it is written by an honoured practical man of the theatre.

Bombast and Sentiment dominate the first half of the eighteenth century theatre. Both are abundantly demonstrated in this 1749 engraving of Quin as Coriolanus. Quin was a man of no little humour; but, apparently, neither he nor his audiences saw anything ridiculous in this costume. The engraving is no malicious caricature but shows the mood of the times by regarding his costume and stance to be as normal as that of the aggrieved ladies. (*Copyright British Museum*)

CHAPTER SIX

Eighteenth Century Theatre

The men and women who were now climbing assiduously into the middle class and wished to be thought aristocratic found it fashionable to go to the theatre. With the help of a new breed of writers who wrote not about life but about writing, they set about creating an atmosphere in marked contrast to the varying improprieties of the Jacobean and Caroline court theatres. What they created was a wordy entertainment called the Theatre of Sentiment, and later the Legitimate Drama. The lower classes gave their encouragement to a very unwordy and strange hybrid entertainment that evolved out of the scenic elaborations of the Masque and the influence of the visiting *Commedia dell'Arte* players, and which became known as Pantomime. By the turn of the next century these were joined by the melodramas and these came to be known as the Illegitimate Drama. It has to be said that the bastard was, in this case, born of love and proved to be a healthy, strapping creature and very good company. While the Legitimate child, more than a little in-bred, proved to be something of an abortion.

The middle-class people and the theatre had been strangers to one another for nearly one hundred years. When, fretted by their long abstention, they went courting again, their conversation was all an evasion and a pretence; they kept their bodies firmly away from each other and sought the imagined safety of an encounter Limited to a Genteel Decorum. No feelings passed between them—they merely Exchanged Protestations couched in Terms of the Utmost Propriety. Life was not to be their God, but Deportment; and feeling underwent a like subjugation to a Curriculum of Correct Sentiment. To breed was not their goal, but to be Well-bred. They buckled on their stays and, thus strait-laced and safely entrenched, gave birth to lots of little words with monstrous big heads. The Capital Letter adorned each high-sounding boneless sentence.

83

There's Consolation when a Friend laments us, but
When a Parent grieves, the Anguish is too native,
Too much our own to be called Pity.
Oh! Sir, consider, I was born to die—
'Tis but expanding Thought, and Life is nothing;
Ages and Generations pass away,
And with resistless Force, like Waves o'er Waves,
Roul down th'irrevocable Stream of Time,
Into the insatiate Ocean for ever—Thus we are gone.

This is not from Tragedy, but from the moral end of an esteemed Comedy—Steele's *The Lying Lover*. ('Oh! That I had lived in good King somebody's Days' sighs the more honest heroine of another comedy.) If comedy could be thus superlative in declamatory images, we may well wonder—was there anything left that tragedy could say? There was. Cibber like Steele is nearer the best than the worst in the prevailing style and his Xerxes may fairly be quoted as typical:

XERXES: Th' injurious sun, the Seas and Wind that saw,
            That sunk and scatter'd my Stupendious Navy,
            Shall feel the Vengeance of a rouzing Deity.
            Give Order that the Wind receive three hundred Lashes. . . .
            Away, draw out an Able Band of Archers,
            Mount 'em on the Battlements of yon lofty Tower,
            And let 'em shoot a thousand Arrows 'gainst the Sun. . . .
            Prepare a hundred Bars of vast hot glaring Iron,
            Then plunge them hissing down
            Into the burning Bowels of the Deep. . . .

Cibber's mad hero brooks little interruption from the Wise Man who comments 'While frantick Passions talk so wild and loud, The Voice of Reason is of little Force':

XERXES: . . . Begone, ye expensive Lumber of the World!

                        A Shout at a Distance

CLEONTES: Behold, great Sir! a thousand skilful Archers,
            From yon high spacious Tower,
            Aloud proclaiming War against the Sun:
            They brace their stubborn Bows, and look
            Resolv'd to make their Arrows reach him.

                        Thunder

XERXES: By Jove they're there!

This is 'expensive lumber' indeed. And if the bathos of the final line is unduly apparent to modern ears, we may be sure that there were some whose healthy laughter must have burst aloud when they heard the like of Rowe's incautious *Calista*:

Is it the voice of thunder, or my Father?

Small wonder that it became, as Whincop relates, 'a Time when it was the fashion to condemn them all, right or wrong, without being heard; and when Parties were made to go to new Plays to make Uproars, which they called by the odious Name of *The Funn of the First Night* . . . one single Word was not heard that the actors spoke . . . however the Actors went thro' it, and the Spectators might see their Mouths wag, and that was all'.

Drury Lane was the temple of the legitimate drama and, after many vicissitudes, its management had passed to a Triumvirate of actors—the foppish Cibber, Wilks (the original Sir Harry Wildair) and Doggett, the low comedian, who kept an eagle eye on the account-books. For twenty years the theatre enjoyed a period of relative good order. Addison's *Cato*, 'a compound of transcendent beauties and absurdity', was an early success and led to the establishment of Barton Booth as Betterton's successor and leading tragedian. Soon, he took over Doggett's share of the management. (Doggett, a shrewd investor, died rich, bequeathing the Coat and Badge that still bear his name, and are rowed for by Thames watermen to this day.) The beautiful Ann Oldfield succeeded Mrs Bracegirdle as leading lady. She was the first to play Rowe's *Jane Shore*, which held the stage throughout the cen-

Fine gentleman and low comedian

Wilks and Doggett—two of the 'triumvirate' of actors who ruled Drury Lane in the early eighteenth century. Wilks, here seen as Wildair in *The Constant Couple* (he was the first to play the part) was 'the perfect type of easy gentleman' and a great pourer of oil on the troubled waters of actors' disputations. Doggett, here seen dancing the Cheshire Round (the only known portrait) was the Low Comedian—and kept the accounts

Genteel Cibber and vulgar Rich

Cibber is here shown as the Fop in excelsis in Vanbrugh's *The Relapse*, engraved by J. Simon from Grisoni's portrait in the Garrick Club. Rich is here shown as Harlequin, in which role he was without rival. (*Author's collection*)

tury and later became one of Mrs Siddon's major roles. This and many similar plays of the time—'She-tragedies' as they have been called—displayed the new actresses to the new feminine element in the audience, all athirst for a good cry in a good cause.

The rival theatre, the theatre that catered for the lower classes, was managed by John Rich, as much an epitome of his audience as Cibber was of his. Cibber was well educated and went on the stage against the wishes of his family. Rich had no education but that of a showman and was bequeathed a theatre by his father. Cibber wrote well and became master of a Foppish wit. Rich was unlettered and his language was vulgar and ungrammatical. Cibber was something of a snob and was hell-bent on being received into High Society. Rich didn't greatly care for anyone's society and developed into an eccentric recluse. 'There's nothing in it to coerce my passions' said Cibber on rejecting a play and filled his theatre with the stiff and over-padded declamatory drama. 'Mr, there is too much *horse-hair* in your tragedy' said Rich. Laughter, something of a rude intruder in such worthy company as the comedies of sentiment, found itself without a voice. Promptly it took to its heels, and somersaulted off into Rich's Harlequinade.

Critical histories of the drama tend to be written by men of letters and there has been much spilling of ink about pantomimes degrading the theatre. This is as priggish as denying toys to children or insisting that laughter must have a purpose. Proper relaxation aside, there is often much pertinent comment of life in the dumb oratory of a good clown—more indeed, than one finds in the starched spoken comedies of the time. Rich's Harlequin drew the common man back to the theatre and the sensibly vulgar atmosphere they created together laid the ground for the truer plays to come.

86

The Pantomimes Groups of Italian comedians in the *Commedia dell'Arte* style had been visiting England with increasing success during the preceding two centuries. Their stock characters found their way into many an English play—Shakespeare's 'Pistol', for example, is as much modelled on the *Commedia* 'Captain' as on life. They appear also, in the early days of the century, under their own names, Harlequin and the like, in home-grown playlets written round their escapades. But, under Rich, they underwent a strange mutation. They lost their voices and told their stories in dumb-show. At a time when much of society was perplexed as to just what was the right thing to say, Rich found the right thing to do.

> Shakespeare, Rowe, Jonson, they are quite undone,
> These are thy Triumphs, thy Exploits, O Lun.

Lun was the stage name adopted by Rich when he performed Harlequin, the central figure of the many pantomimes that now flooded the stage and brought 'more Money to the House than all the Poets put together'.

The pantomimes were, at first, given as 'after-pieces' when the more solemn business of the evening was over. There had long been a custom whereby admission to the theatre at reduced rates was permitted after the third act of the tragedy. This attracted the shopkeepers and clerks whose work did not permit their attending before seven o'clock (the performances began at six). Soon the after-pieces were chosen to suit the tastes of this sixpenny audience and, when pantomime had proved its popularity, the price for late-

Eighteenth Century Theatre

The comedy of sentiment and the fun of pantomime

The Tender Husband by Sir Richard Steele (one of the masters of the Comedy of Sentiment) has a frontispiece by Van der Gucht (1735) which finds a very strange echo in an Italian eighteenth century engraving of Harlequin playing the Artist, in which he gives his lady's portrait more than a hint of his own beard. (*Author's collection*)

'A just view of the British stage'

A satire (attributed to Hogarth) on the rage for pantomime, showing the Triumvirate pulling the strings, and the statues of the comic and tragic muses beheaded. (*Author's collection*)

John Gay, author of *The Beggar's Opera*, which 'made Gay rich and Rich gay'. (*Author's collection*)

coming to the pit was increased to a shilling. (Full-time attendance in the pit still cost half-a-crown.)

The pantomimes were a strange compound of ballet and acrobatic clowning which told their stories to the accompaniment of explanatory songs. They ranged far and wide for their subject-matter, pilfering classic myths, contemporary criminal records, and the old stock plays. Mars, Venus, Orpheus, Cupid and Apollo found themselves in strange company with Doctor Faustus and Jack Sheppard, the prison-breaker. Through them all chased Harlequin in pursuit of Columbine and tripping with Punch and Pierrot. The pantomime 'consisted of two parts: one serious, and the other comic' says Davies. 'By the help of gay scenes, fine habits, grand dances, appropriate music, and other decorations' Rich exhibited a story from the fables. 'Between the pauses or acts of this serious representation, he interwove a comic fable, consisting chiefly of the courtship of Harlequin and Columbine, with a variety of surprising adventures and tricks which were produced by the magic wand of Harlequin: such as the sudden transformation of palaces and temples to huts and cottages; of men and women into wheelbarrows and joint-stools; of trees turned into houses; colonnades to beds of tulips; and mechanics' shops into serpents and ostriches'. No other performer equalled Rich as Harlequin: 'His gesticulation was so perfectly expressive of his meaning, that every motion of his hand or head, or any part of his body, was a kind of dumb eloquence that was readily understood by his audience.' He combined clowning antics with the affecting grace of a ballet dancer.

There was considerable grieving by the judicious that the popularity of the pantomimes

Strolling players in a country barn

Painted and engraved by Hogarth in 1838—a graphic illustration of the back-stage chaos inseparable from the conditions of life for the strollers. (*Author's collection*)

was lowering the tone of the theatre. Booth, the foremost tragedian and now one of the Drury Lane management, was approached at a coffee-house by a number of worthy gentlemen. After complimenting him on his excellent acting in the tragedy (as the younger Cibber records the story) 'they jointly (but genteelly) blamed him for having tacked to so fine a play that senseless stuff' (the pantomime), adding that it was 'much beneath the dignity of the theatre'. Mr Booth frankly answered that he thought a thin audience was a much greater indignity. The pantomimes, by adding to the revenue, enabled 'the managers to be more expensive in their habits, and other decorations of the theatre. . . . He could not think it was the business of the directors to be wise to empty boxes'. Over at Drury Lane, Cibber at first sought to dismiss the craze as 'new-fangled foppery' but was soon driven to adopt the 'monstrous medlies'.

The New Writers Societies for the Reformation of Manners dominated the times—and the dramatists seem to have taken out life subscriptions. Life's harum-scarum dance mutated unto a modish minuet; and the drama was Conducted on the Most Elevated Principles. A universal megrim set in, a self-inflicted attack of the vapours—the atmosphere was stifling. John Rich opened the windows and in blustered John Gay, like a rude wind to set the chandeliers tinkling. His blustering *Beggar's Opera*, an unruly Hogarthian compound of farce and political satire, of romance and savagery, swept the town, making 'Gay rich and Rich gay'. In the form of a ballad-opera, the story tells how Macheath, a ruffianly highwayman, threads his boisterous way through a maze of evil pretence. Though the corrupt judge who took bribes, the father-in-law who is both fence and informer, and sundry other fairfaced foul creatures are all topical satire on contemporary villians, the play's comment has proved timeless. (In recent times it has served as model for Brecht's *Three-Penny Opera*.)

The *Beggar's Opera* had not come to ruffle the staid deportment of the legitimate drama until the century was twenty-eight years old. It was a reaction; Fielding's burlesque, *Tom Thumb*, which came two years later, was a direct attack. It ridiculed by parody, by underlining the bathos inherent in all the over-inflated bombast in the fashionable plays. Only a year after this, a quite different kind of dramatist was to take advantage of this invaluable clearing of the ground. In 1731 the Drury Lane audience assembled for a new play, questioning 'the presumption of the author, in hoping to make them sympathize in the

Fielding, a sketch attributed to Hogarth.
(*Author's collection*)

sorrows of any man beneath the rank of emperor, king or statesman'. It told a murder story about ordinary people in the prose of everyday speech. A young apprentice's passion for a whore leads him to robbery and, finally murder; they are both hanged. The author who so boldly forsook the traditional courtly terrain of tragedy was rewarded with an immense success. Lillo's *George Barnwell* was the rage of the town. Five years later he followed it with a better play with a similar background—*The Fatal Curiosity*. Both maintained their popularity for well over a hundred years. Neither play carries much conviction for modern readers but Lillo's influence is of major importance to our drama.

The State of the Theatres Covent Garden Theatre had been built in 1732 and John Rich moved in from Lincoln's Inn Fields where he had been operating for the last eighteen years. Five years later the Licensing Act limited the presentation of plays to Covent Garden and Drury Lane, with Opera at the King's Haymarket (built in 1705). The old theatre in Goodman's Fields and the Little Theatre, in the Haymarket, built in 1720, sought ingenious means of evading the law. Cibber retired in 1733 and Drury Lane entered a period of bad management by men-about-town, many of the actors seceding to the Haymarket Little, of which Fielding became manager for two years, until the pertinence of his satires brought about its closure.

Enter Garrick 'With very little variation of cadence, and in a deep, full tone, accompanied by a sawing kind of action, which had more of the senate than the stage in it, he rolled out his heroics with an air of dignified indifference that seemed to disdain the plaudits that were bestowed upon him.' The actor is Quin, the Prime Minister of Tragedy in the 1740s, the most admired of all the many drones on stilts. The commentator is Richard Cumberland and he is equally evocative in his portrait of the leading lady. 'Mrs Cibber, in a key high-pitched, but sweet withal, sung, or rather recitatived Rowe's harmonious strain. . . .

The young Garrick

Hayman's portrait shows Garrick as Ranger in *The Suspicious Husband*, a part he created in 1747. This illustration shows only a part of the whole picture, which is in the London Museum, and illustrates very clearly the freshness he must have brought to a tired stage. (*Copyright London Museum*)

It was so extremely wanting in contrast that though it did not wound the ear it wearied it; when she had once recited two or three speeches, I could anticipate the manner of every succeeding one—it was like a long legendary ballad of innumerable stanzas, every one of which is sung to the same tune, eternally chiming to the ear without variation or relief.' Reform, long overdue, was soon to come.

In 1741 'a young gentleman who never appeared on any stage' played Richard III at a minor theatre to a few friends and a poor £30-worth of nonchalant time-killers. At the end of the performance the newcomer was greeted with 'loud shouts of approbation'. David Garrick had arrived. In the next seven months he was seen in eighteen different parts. 'Notwithstanding the distance of Goodman's Fields from the *fashionable* part of London, the long space . . . is said to have been nightly blocked up by the carriages of the nobility and gentry.' Quin came to examine this wildfire success: 'If the young fellow is right, I and the rest of the players have all been wrong.' It was not long before Garrick came to Drury Lane and the town was able to judge between the two styles.

'When, after long and eager expectation, I first beheld little Garrick, then young and light, and alive in every muscle and in every feature, come bounding on the stage, and pointing at . . . the heavy-paced Horatio (Quin), Heavens, what a transition! It seemed as if a whole century had been stepped over in the changing of a single scene—old things were done away, and a new order at once brought forward.' Cumberland wrote this in recollection, but a newspaper report of the time is more explicit in contrasting the new and the old. Garrick's voice was 'sweet and harmonious, without monotony, drawling or affectation: it was neither whining, bellowing, nor grumbling, but perfectly easy in its transitions, natural in its cadence, and beautiful in its elocution. He is not less happy in his mien and gait, in which he is neither strutting nor mincing, neither stiff nor slouching. When three or four are on the stage with him, he is attentive to whatever is spoke, and never drops his character when he has finished a speech, by either looking contemptuously on an inferior performer, unnecessary spitting, or suffering his eyes to wander through the whole circle of spectators'.

Few actors have earned such lengthy eulogies as Garrick but, alas, most are pure panegyric. One of the most concise is perhaps one of the most revealing. Kitty Clive was watching him from the wings, still smarting from some rebuke that had exasperated her: 'Damn him, he could act a *grid-iron*.' (A grid-iron was the very solid wooden structure above the stage from which scenery was suspended.) What distinguishes him most from his rivals in all ages is that he was as supreme in comedy as in tragedy. His audiences could see him play *King Lear* and, later in the same evening, *Abel Drugger*, his comic masterpiece, in which 'his appalled look of terror where he drops the glass drew as much applause from the audience as his Lear had done'. Lear was commonly held to be his best performance in tragedy, though Hamlet received great praise. Not the least revealing tribute comes, obliquely, from the naïve Partridge in Fielding's novel *Tom Jones*: 'He the best player! Why I could act as well myself. I am sure, if I had seen a ghost, I should have looked in the very same manner, and had done just as he did . . . the King for my money; he speaks all his words distinctly, half as loud again as the others—anybody may see he's an actor.'

Amongst so much praise, King George's 'he was a great fidget' has value. Much of

Garrick in four of his characters

(1) In female attire as Sir John Bruce in *The Provok'd Wife* (J. Roberts, 1776)
(2) As Abel Drugger boxing his own reflection in a mirror. Unsigned etching
(3) As King Lear (Terry, 1779)
(4) As Macbeth (Parkinson, 1775). (*All author's collection*)

Macklin as Shylock

This portrait of the actor is taken from a large stipple engraving by Nutter after Boyne. (*Author's collection*)

Peg Woffington in breeches

This print is variously described as representing her in *The Female Volunteer* and *The Constant Couple—* as Sir Harry Wildair. (*Author's collection*)

Garrick's power to please an audience was gained by his physical grace, apt gesture and byplay—not for nothing had he seen (and even, on occasion, performed) Harlequin. But it was a novelty at the time to employ these legitimate extensions of the actor's powers beyond the statuesque pose and strut then fashionable. Were his actions as natural as his speech, or did they grow, in time, to be more concerned with making arresting 'effects'?

'Garrick is a new religion. Whitefield was followed for a time; but they will all come to church again' said Quin. Garrick replied in an apt verse:

> When Doctrines meet with gen'ral approbation,
> It is not Heresy, but Reformation.

To give Garrick credit for the whole reformation of acting is to do something less than justice to his friend, Macklin. Some eight months earlier Macklin had startled his colleagues at Drury lane with a very new Shylock. The tradition at the time was to play the part as a low-comedy clown in a red wig and tattered clothes, as Doggett had done in an earlier very free adaptation that treated the action as farce. Macklin restored the Shakespeare text, dressed the part correctly and played Shylock as a villain in a naturalistic manner. He 'spoke so familiar, and so little in the hoity-toity tone of the Tragedy of that day' that he must have made an astonishing contrast to Quin, ranting as Antonio.

Macklin in his early forties was the roughest of diamonds. 'If God Almighty writes a legible hand, that man must be a villain' said Quin. The Wild Irishman's appearance was

Green Room Scuffle　　This Gillray caricature shows Peg Woffington and Kitty Clive at blows back-stage. (*Author's collection*)

strikingly savage. Bursting with energy, he was impetuous to a fault, generous in friendship and very dangerous in enmity. He and the dapper, sprightly young Garrick were great friends, Macklin unstinting with advice and encouragement, and both aflame with zeal to reform. They set up house together, and Peg Woffington came to join them.

Because she had 'so charming a figure and so handsome a person' Rich, at Covent Garden, had given Woffington a trial. 'Her choice of character excited the public. Sir Harry Wildair acted by a woman was a novelty. This gay, dissipated, good-humoured rake she represented with so much ease, elegance and propriety of deportment, that no male actor has since equalled her in that part.' Coming into the Green Room, dressed as Sir Harry, she said one night: 'In my conscience! I believe half the men in the house take me for one of their own sex.' Quin tartly replied that he was sure that the other half could convince them to the contrary. To what Arthur Murphy engagingly calls her 'one female error' must be added that she 'possessed captivating charms as a jovial, witty bottle companion', being the only woman admitted into one of the essentially male strongholds, the Beef-steak Club, of which she is even said to have been elected President.

Garrick was very much in love with her; at first wanted to marry her; then didn't; and finally broke company with her. Then he and Macklin quarrelled over an involved dispute with the management who were defaulting on salaries. There were faults on both sides but it was Macklin who suffered worst, losing employment for some time to come.

Garrick continued to add to his fame in a variety of parts and eventually, in 1747, became manager of Drury Lane. 'Like a true politician,' Garrick 'neither loved nor hated

SARAH SIDDONS—This sketch of the actress when young by Romney is in the Ashmolean Museum, Oxford. *Copyright Ashmolean Museum.*

EDMUND KEAN—Clint's sketch in oils of Kean has been chosen because it brings us so much more of the actor's arresting magic than any painter has caught of Garrick's more elusive characteristics. It portrays Kean as Sir Giles Overreach in Massinger's "A New Way to Pay Old Debts". *Copyright Victoria and Albert Museum.*

(a)
A Riot at
Covent Garden,
1763.

(b)
Scene from
"The Beggar's Opera",
1790.

(a) shows a performance of "Artaxerxes" at Covent Garden interrupted by the audience rioting
Beggar's Opera". *Copyright Tate Gallery.* (c) shows Skelt's famous Twopenny Coloured print of "T
Piper's sketch for the Olivier "Oedipus

(c)
Scene from
"The Miller and
His Men",
1813.

(d)
Scene from
"Oedipus Rex",
John Piper.

ed admission charges. *Author's collection.* (b) reproduces Hogarth's painting of a scene from "The
Men". *Author's collection.* (d) shows the work of one of our foremost present-day artists—John
Vic in 1945. *Courtesy of John Piper.*

Bernard Shaw—Augustus John's portrait celebrates our remembrance of our leading 20th century dramatist. *Copyright Fitzwilliam Museum, Cambridge.*

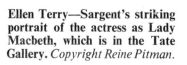

Ellen Terry—Sargent's striking portrait of the actress as Lady Macbeth, which is in the Tate Gallery. *Copyright Reine Pitman.*

in the way of business' and he welcomed Macklin back to the company. The quarrel, however, proved to be only temporarily patched, not mended, and soon Macklin left to pursue further quarrels and nurture a genius for litigation.

> . . . The drama's laws the drama's patrons give,
> For we, who live to please, must please to live. . . .
> 'Tis yours this night to bid the reign commence
> Of rescued nature and reviving sense.

Dr Johnson wrote the prologue to Garrick's new season and Garrick spoke it. The theatre had received much-needed redecoration, the company was the very strongest Garrick could recruit, and the whole enterprise was subject to proper authority and a sensible discipline. All parts had to be properly learnt (no one permitted to 'supply the defect by a bold front and forging matter of their own') and there must be proper and punctual attendance at rehearsals.

'Wignell, why can't you say "Mr Strickland, your coach is ready" as an ordinary man would say it, and not with the declamatory pomp of Mr Quin playing tyrants?' 'Sir,' said poor Wignell, 'I thought in that passage I *had* kept down the sentiment.' For thirty years Garrick drove and taught. It was more often than not an unruly crew and he got little thanks for his pains. Not the least vexatious of his leading ladies was Kitty Clive but her generous letter to him when he eventually retired gives a vivid picture of his reign. 'In the height of the public admiration for you . . . when they were admiring everything you did . . . I was a living witness that they did not know, nor could they be sensible of half your perfections. I have seen you with your magic hammer in your hand, endeavouring to beat your ideas into the heads of creatures, who had none of their own. I have seen you, with lamb-like patience, endeavouring to make them comprehend you; and I have seen you, when that could not be done, I have seen your lamb turned into a lion; by this your great labour and pains, the public was entertained; *they* thought they all acted very fine; they did not see you pull the wires.'

Garrick's mercurial character in private life emerges vividly from Leslie's *Life of Reynolds*: 'The most perfect type of the actor. Quick in sympathy, vivid in observation . . . delighted to give delight, and spurred to ever higher effort by the reflection of the effect produced on others—no matter whether his audience were the crowd of an applauding theatre, a table full of noblemen and wits, a nursery group of children, or a solitary black boy in an area; of inordinate vanity—at once the most courteous, genial, sore, and sensitive of men; full of kindliness and yet ever quarrelling; scheming for applause even in the society of his most intimate friends.'

Garrick's Players Much of Garrick's success was due to the strength of the acting talent with which he surrounded himself. Besides Woffington, he started with three leading ladies. Mrs Cibber, delightful and insinuating, the commanding Mrs Pritchard (his Lady Macbeth) and Kitty Clive who trod the stage in an easy manner 'as if at home' and was unparalleled in comedy's romps and hoydens. Bellamy came later to bring more youthful charms than

Garrick's actresses

(1) Abington, the supreme arbiter of feminine fashion, as Lady Betty Modish in *The Careless Husband*. (I. Taylor 1777)

(2) Cibber in *The Orphan*. (Thornthwaite 1776)

(3) Bellamy, Garrick's Juliet, as the Comic Muse (Coates/Bartollozi 1785)

(4) Pritchard as Lady Macbeth (Zoffany/Green 1776). She was undeniably the first great tragic actress the British stage has seen. (*All author's collection*)

ability to her Juliet, and to reveal a talent for elopement (sometimes in the middle of a performance). And Abington, who rose from tavern flower-girl to become the supreme arbiter of feminine fashion. Among the men, handsome Spranger Barry provided serious rivalry to Garrick himself—a better Othello and at least as good a Romeo. Their Juliet commented that whereas she thought Garrick would have jumped into her balcony, she thought she must have jumped out of it to the silver-voiced Barry. Later Quin came back and let his own generous conviviality and wit shine on his one memorably natural performance as Falstaff to Garrick's Hotspur.

Garrick's Reforms In the seventies Garrick imported the scenic artist de Loutherbourg from the continent to enliven the pantomimes with realistic fires, volcanoes in eruption and dramatic cloud-effects. Of more serious and lasting worth were his use of built-up settings to replace the formal cloth and wings then in vogue, his use of perspective, and the new variety and control he achieved over stage lighting.

Garrick regarded himself as a supreme purist in the matter of restoring an uncorrupted Shakespeare text, claiming that he 'lost no drop of that immortal man'. This was as much vain nonsense as was his promotion of the Shakespeare Jubilee at Stratford, a resolute three-day programme of odes, songs, speeches and loyal effusions, distinguished by the complete absence of anything by Shakespeare—and by the wrath of the heavens, which opened to swamp the earnest dullness of the proceedings in judicious cloudfalls of rain. Among his 'improvements' to the Shakespeare plays may be noticed the crowding out of Bottom and the rustics from *The Dream* to permit the addition of twenty-five songs to Shakespeare's modest three. His version of *Hamlet* 'rescued that noble play from all the rubbish of the fifth act'. Out went the gravediggers, the fencing match, the death of Rosencrantz and Guildenstern, the death of Ophelia, the poisoning of the Queen (led out, mad from remorse, instead). This left him a clear stage to die heroically and at a greater length than the parsimonious Shakespeare had envisaged.

Garrick introduced a number of necessary reforms among his audience. He abolished their old right of 'tasting' a play and demanding their money back on leaving at the end of the first act. He attempted to abolish entrance for half-price after act three, but gave up when this led to damaging riots. Best of all he abolished spectators from the stage itself. Actors depended greatly for their earnings on the profits of their benefit nights and 'building on the stage' had long been a method of augmenting the accommodation on these occasions. Tate Wilkinson gives us a graphic description of what the practice led to in the 1760s:

Suppose an audience behind the curtain up to the clouds, with persons of a menial cast on the ground, beaux and no-beaux crowding the only entrance, what a play it must have been whenever Romeo was breaking open the supposed tomb, which was no more than a screen on those nights set up, and Mrs Cibber prostrating herself on an old black couch, covered with black cloth, as the tomb of the Capulets, with at least (on a great benefit-night) two hundred persons behind her, which formed the background . . . a performer on a popular night could not step his foot with safety, lest he either should thereby hurt or offend, or be thrown down amongst scores of idle, tipsy apprentices.

Eighteenth Century Theatre

99

When Garrick abolished this custom, he was able to compensate the actors for the loss of the £100 to £150 it brought them by increasing the size of the auditorium.

It would be pleasant to record that Garrick extended his reforms to choosing better new plays—but such was not the case. Though his own ephemeral writings, his odd verses, prologues and epilogues are not without distinction, his own plays and those he chose are little better than run-of-the-mill.

Garrick retired in 1776 after a series of farewell performances of his greatest roles that moved the town to an hysteria of adulation. On his death he was buried in Westminster Abbey and earned from Dr Johnson the enviable epitaph: 'I am disappointed by that stroke of death which has eclipsed the gaiety of nations and impoverished the public stock of harmless pleasure.'

Re-enter the Dramatists The Comedies of Sentiment were written 'not to imitate the manners, but to reform the morals of the age' and, as Hazlitt says, 'nothing can be better meant, or more inefficient. It is almost a misnomer to call them comedies; they are rather homilies in dialogue, in which a number of very pretty ladies and gentlemen discuss the fashionable topics . . . with a sickly sensibility. . . . The whole distinction between virtue and vice . . . is reduced to verbal professions, and a mechanical, infantine goodness. . . . The comic writer . . . ought to open the volume of nature and the world for his living materials, and not take them out of his ethical common-place book'. A glance at the plays

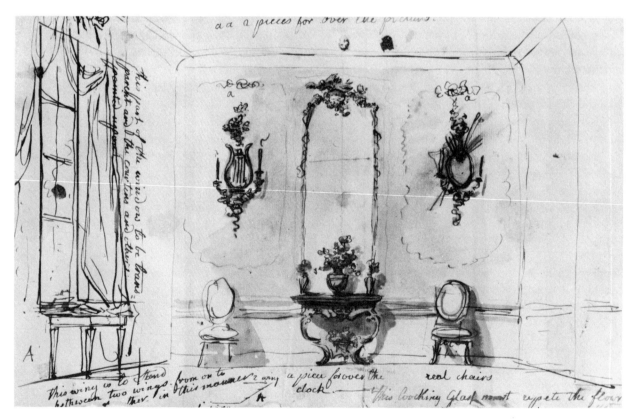

A stage design by de Loutherbourg, Garrick's Designer. The original is in the author's collection, but it has not as yet been possible to attribute the design to a particular play. It is important as illustrating a number of devices new to the time

arrick in later years. An original pencil-drawing by orlidge. (*Author's collection*)

Goldsmith from an engraving by Macki of Sir Joshua Reynold's painting 1777. (*Author's collection*)

proves his point. 'How unnecessary is Thought!' says Taverner's Lord Absent in *The Artful Wife*, 'What Confusion has it occasion'd! What Animosities has it rais'd in the World.' Lady Absent is equally given to moral meditation—'How delightful is the Matrimonial State, when two Minds have but one Desire! . . . Methinks there should be but few bad women, Virtue is so delightful.'

'Band-box' says Goldsmith's Lumpkin 'all a made up thing' and sends the whole flimsy artifice reeling. A spectator, his sentiments nicely regulated by seventy years of comedy proliferating in Politeness of Style and Genteelness of Expression, must have met with a very rude shock when Goldsmith's *She Stoops to Conquer* came along in 1773. Attending the first night must have been like sitting in the middle of a revolution. The play is not one page old before it declares a genial homely reality utterly alien to the stage of the time. Mr and Mrs Hardcastle are enjoying an amiable wrangle:

MRS H.   Here we live in an old rambling mansion, that looks for the all the world like an inn, but that we never see company. Our best visitors are old Mrs Oddfish, the curate's wife, and little Cripplegate, the lame dancing master: and all our entertainment your old stories of Prince Eugene and the Duke of Marlborough. I hate such old-fashioned trumpery.

MR H.   And I love it. I love everything that's old: old friends, old times, old manners, old books, old wine; and I believe, Dorothy, you'll own I have been pretty fond of an old wife.   101

'She Stoops to
Conquer',
Act V, Sc. 1

A scene from the play, painted by T. Parkinson, engraved by W. Humphrey,
showing Shuter, Mrs Green and Quick as Mr and Mrs Hardcastle and Tony
Lumpkin in the original production. (*Copyright British Museum*)

MRS H.   Lord, Mr Hardcastle, you're for ever at your Dorothys and your old wives. You may
be a Darby, but I'll be no Joan, I promise you. I'm not so old as you'd make me, by
more than one good year. Add twenty to twenty, and make money of that.

MR H.   Let me see; twenty added to twenty, makes just fifty and seven.

And so the play proceeds with its story of endearingly real people, rumbustious and uninhibited, 'warts and all', who keep their truth of speech no matter what farcical absurd-
ities the action may rattle them into. The boisterous lumpy bumpkin may kick and prance
like a foal let fresh into the field, but he's full of good horse-sense. His animal spirits are
neatly contrasted with the young townee's lack of assurance when faced with 'all the terrors
of a formal courtship'. With what a sense of shock and relief must the audience have welcomed a hero who could only stutter his sentiments. That he can only loose his tongue when
the girl throws off her starched sentiments and speaks plain chambermaid is a master-
stroke of irony that could only have had its fullest force with an audience long satiated
with heroes who had a word for everything and a heart for nothing. It is a glorious play,
written in glorious English. When oak is out of fashion and diamonds are in, it may seem
inelegant; but its durability is assured. At last an eighteenth century dramatist has let us
see the men behind the wigs.

On Garrick's retirement, the control of Drury Lane passed to Sheridan. With Colman
at Covent Garden, this meant that both theatres were in the hands of writers. Sheridan is as
different from Goldsmith as wit is from humour but his demolishment of the Moral Precep-

102

Sheridan—good and bad. His wit and easy charm enabled his friends to think of him as Reynolds painted him (*left*). Gillray's savage caricature (*right*) is one of many that show what his enemies thought of his heavy drinking and passionate carelessness with other people's money. (*Author's collection*)

'**The School for Scandal**'—The Screen Scene—Drury Lane 1777. This illustrates an actual scene from the first production. (*Copyright Victoria and Albert Museum*)

tors is no less drastic. The kind of sentimental utterance that Goldsmith so happily sent stuttering forms a fit preface to Sheridan's very different mode of demolishing the century's men of deportment. 'And now Fidelia' cries Moore's Belmont in *The Foundling*, 'What you have made me, take me—a Convert to Honour! I have at last learnt, that Custom can be no authority for Vice; and however the mistaken World may judge, he who solicits Pleasure, at the Expense of Innocence, is the Vilest of Betrayers.' The key-words are there, epitomizing the whole dialogue of counsel that pervades every last act's inevitable moralizing. 'He who....' 'He who....' The witty Irishman wrote a whole play round them. When the screen falls in *The School for Scandal* and Joseph Surface is exposed, some seventy years of sanctimonious humbugs are put to rout. Flustered at last, Joseph attempts to take refuge in he-whoing but the game is up, and he has to run from the stage. Did the audience, wearied by seventy years of canting, hypocritical heroes, think that these, too, would now quit their stage? The applause at the final curtain on the first night made such a noise and a vibration that a passing journalist ran for his life, lest the building should fall.

The School for Scandal was seen at Drury Lane in 1777. Two years before, Sheridan's play, *The Rivals*, had been seen at Covent Garden and this, after revision, became an enduring success. In the same year Sheridan produced a comic opera, *The Duenna*, the most unaccountably neglected of our theatre's masterpieces. It held the stage for just so long as every dramatic company automatically included a corps of competent actor-singers, and should not now be lost to audiences solely because it fails to fit comfortably into the present-day repertoire of either our dramatic or operatic companies.

Sheridan's last comedy, *The Critic*, lineal descendant of Fielding's *Tom Thumb* (and the earlier *The Rehearsal* by Buckingham), burlesques the old-style plays and the new-style critics. It also gave Sheridan, the manager, a chance to exploit the attractions lent by lavish scenery and costumes.

A bare six years had seen the advent of five masterpieces—from Goldsmith's *She Stoops to Conquer* in 1773 to Sheridan's *The Critic* in 1779. There had been no plays of like stature since Farquhar's *The Beaux' Stratagem* some seventy years before; and it would be some hundred and twenty years before a third Irishman, Oscar Wilde, provided any serious rivalry. The six years stand like an oasis in the long desert of nearly two hundred years, and we are left wondering why, given this new lease of life, our drama remained barren of distinction for so very long.

Re-enter the Actors The last days of 1775 had seen *The Merchant of Venice* on the bill at Drury Lane, with Portia by 'A young Lady—Her first appearance'. Overcome by nerves, the young provincial actress made the poorest showing and was roundly damned by the critics. When, after a further five years in the provinces, Mrs Siddons faced London again in 1782, she became established overnight as 'the first tragic actress now on the English stage'. The public was infatuated with her, the whole town talked of little else. 'To have seen Mrs Siddons' wrote Hazlitt, 'was an event in everyone's life.' Her brother, John Kemble, joined her the following year and together they remained at the head of the profession until her retirement thirty years later in 1812.

'If you ask me, What is a Queen? I should say Mrs Siddons' says Tate Wilkinson.

Sarah Siddons as Lady Macbeth, from a wax bust in the National Gallery of Ireland. (*Copyright National Gallery of Ireland*)

Siddons rehearsing in the Green Room, with Henderson and her father, Roger Kemble, from a drawing by Rowlandson. (*Author's collection*)

Silhouette of Mrs Siddons in Rowe's *Jane Shore*.
(*Author's collection*)

'She was not less than a goddess or a prophetess inspired by the gods . . . she was Tragedy personified' says Hazlitt. 'It was the magnificent countenance of an animated statue . . . more than regal—say rather, immortal' says John Wilson, ' . . . none knew the troubled grandeur of guilt till they saw her in Lady Macbeth, walking in her sleep. . . . Shakespeare's self had learned something then from a sight of Siddons.' The eulogies have such an insistence on grandeur that one is tempted to wonder if she lacked life. 'I have read all the high-flown descriptions of the critics, and they fall short. I want you to tell me in plain blunt phrase just what impression she produced on you.' The questioner is the American tragedian, Edwin Forrest and he is talking about her sleep-walking scene to the English dramatist Sheridan Knowles who replied, 'with a sort of shudder. . . . Well, sir, I smelt blood! I swear that I smelt blood'. Siddons, it is apparent, was not all marble magnificence; the epic creature had a heart and a galvanic poetic imagination that conjured up a huge range of emotions in her auditors, yet 'never indulged in imagination at the expense of truth'.

Boaden, her biographer, gives us a valuable physical description of her in the days of her early triumphs. 'Her height is above the middle size, but not at all inclined to the *embonpoint*; there is, notwithstanding, nothing sharp or angular in the frame; there is sufficient muscle to bestow a roundness upon the limbs, and her attitudes are, therefore, distinguished equally by energy and grace.' The features of her face are 'finely formed, though strong', neither coarse nor unfeminine. 'So great, too, is the flexibility of her coun-

tenance, that the rapid transitions of passion are given with a variety and effect that never

Kemble as Hamlet in Paris 1827, from a litho by H. Gaugain. Also in this picture of the play is Miss Smithson (as Ophelia) who later married the composer Berlioz. (*Author's collection*)

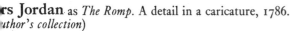
rs **Jordan** as *The Romp*. A detail in a caricature, 1786. (*Author's collection*)

Cooke engraved by Rogers. (*Author's collection*)

tire upon the eye. Her voice is naturally plaintive, and a tender melancholy in her level speaking denotes a being devoted to tragedy; yet this seemingly settled quality of voice becomes at will sonorous or piercing, overwhelms with rage, or in its wild shriek absolutely harrows up the soul. Her sorrow, too, is never childish; her lamentation has a dignity which belongs, I think, to no other woman; it claims your respect along with your tears.'

John Philip Kemble made his first appearance in London at Drury Lane in 1783 as Hamlet. Henderson, fostered by Garrick, was the reigning tragedian at the time, and a friend, Richard Sharp, wrote to him: 'There has not been such a first appearance since yours; yet nature, though she has been bountiful to him in figure and features, has denied him a voice. Now and then he was as deliberate in his delivery as if he had been reading prayers, and had waited for the responses. He is a very handsome man, almost tall, and almost large, with features of a sensible, but fixed and tragic cast. His action is graceful, though somewhat formal. . . . Very careful study appears in all he says and does; but there is more singularity and ingenuity than simplicity and fire.' A memoir in a magazine at the time of his death points out that 'Mr Kemble did not, like his sister, burst on the town in the full maturity of his powers. He was a gentleman and a scholar, with signal advantages of person, and with almost equal defects of voice, who determined to become a noble actor, and who succeeded by infinite perseverance and care, assisted doubtless by the reputation and influence of Mrs Siddons. He formed a high standard in his own mind, and gradually rose to its level . . . he went on calmly studying the principles of his art, and succeeded at last in presenting the stateliest pictures of Roman greatness, and giving the most approp-

'A wilderness of a place' said Mrs Siddons of the 1794 Drury Lane. This water colour by Edward Dayes of the interior during a performance abundantly illustrates how much the actors would have to magnify their effects to dominate the huge auditorium (seating 3,600 people—500 more than the present Drury Lane). (*Agnew Art Gallery and Huntingdon Art Gallery*)

riate expression to philosophic thought, that it had entered into modern imagination to conceive'. Haydon perhaps best hits off his stiffness: 'Kemble came into a part with a stately dignity, as if he disdained to listen to nature, however she did whisper, until he had examined and weighed the value of her counsel.' That there was more than a little of the wit lurking behind the statuesque toga of the classic tragedian is evident from the following endearing anecdote of Moore's: 'One night, when John Kemble was performing at some country theatre one of his most favourite parts, he was much interrupted, from time to time, by the squalling of a young child in one of the galleries. At length, angered by this rival performance, Kemble walked with solemn step to the front of the stage, and addressing the audience in his most tragic tones, said "Ladies and Gentlemen, unless the play is stopped, the child cannot possibly go on." '

Two years after Kemble's début, Mrs Jordan made her first appearance in London in Garrick's *The Country Girl*, an adaptation of Wycherley's *The Country Wife*. Mrs Jordan 'ran upon the stage as a playground, and laughed from sincere wildness of delight'. Hazlitt says 'she gave more pleasure than any other actress, because she had the greatest spirit of enjoyment in herself . . . her smile had the effect of sunshine . . . it seemed as if her heart were always at her mouth. She was all gaiety, openness, and good nature; she rioted in her fine animal spirits'. The country girls, the tomboys, the romps and hoydens, had never held such charm and delight as she gave them. Her infectious high spirits and the beauty of her figure carried her triumphantly through Sir Harry Wildair and the other 'breeches' parts that it was still the fashion for actresses to play. More than all this, she found the tenderness at the heart of Shakespeare's Viola and Rosalind. 'There is no giving an account how she delivered the disguised story of her love for Orsino' says Lamb, 'she used no rhetoric in her passion; or it was nature's own rhetoric, most legitimate then, when it seemed altogether without rule or law.' She was the embodiment of the Comic Muse, painted as such, and remembered as pre-eminent among all our actresses in comedy.

In 1800 George Frederick Cooke appeared at Covent Garden as Richard III, with such marked success that Kemble never thereafter played the part for fear of the comparison. For ten years Cooke's powerful thirst threw a bewildered management into abundant consternation. He was often drunk to the point of madness and the theatre never knew whether he would arrive in time, or, indeed, if he would arrive at all. On his night, there is little doubt that he was magnificent. Kean admired him greatly and erected a monument to him in New York, whither Cooke had gone to find initial triumph; then neglect when he grew undependable; and finally an inglorious death.

Well, as you guess:.

The Theatrical Atlas—Cruikshank's famous cartoon (1814) with Kean as Richard III, celebrates his deliverance of Drury Lane from the doldrums into which it had sunk before his much-needed arrival. (*Author's collection*)

CHAPTER SEVEN

Nineteenth Century Theatre

Early Nineteenth Century 'Grandiose' is the key-word at the turn of the century. It is inherent in the characters of Siddons and Kemble and becomes even more apparent as they settle into their mould. And the characteristic is sadly and monstrously aggravated when the old intimate theatres are rebuilt. 'A wilderness of a place' said Mrs Siddons of the 1794 Drury Lane, in which the original accommodation for two thousand people had been increased to three thousand six hundred. (Some five hundred more than our own present-day very spacious Drury Lane.) Covent Garden, rebuilt in 1809 after fire, accommodated little short of three thousand. In these two huge theatres, cavernous and ill-lit, the actors struggled to magnify their effects to overcome the constant complaints that they could neither be seen nor be heard properly—and in an attempt to gain authority over a new audience increasingly given to tumult and disorder. This led to a concentration on pageantry and spectacle, plays with a minimum of simple dialogue and a maximum of violent action supported by all the resources of sensationalism, glittering costumes and spectacular scenic effects. Grandiose staging, grandiose acting, and the hollow ring of grandiosity in the new plays.

Into this atmosphere of artificiality there erupted an actor of volcanic force—Edmund Kean. 'To see Kean act,' said Coleridge, was 'like reading Shakespeare by flashes of lightning.' He found the breadth of effect necessary to fill the huge theatres and yet, despite the violence of his performances, he found too, a kind of reality that made Kemble seem stuffed and stagey. 'At his first step on the London stage he was acknowledged to be the founder of a new school.' He came, adds the memoir in Blackwood's Magazine— 'to refresh the feelings and change the worship of those who had for a quarter of a century bowed down to the supremacy of the Kembles'.

Kean was a hungry fighter. He had known 'a birth and youth of poverty and desertion —for he never seems to have known who his father was, and even his mother's identity was doubtful'. His ragamuffin boyhood was spent playing truant in and out of the theatres. At nine he played Robin, the page, in *The Merry Wives* at Drury Lane. At sixteen, as 'Master Carey', he recited at Covent Garden and, at seventeen he played (for fifteen shillings a week) a season of leading parts at Sheerness. The ten years between then and his sudden success were spent gathering a variety of experience ranging from intermittent destitution as a stroller to his final regular employment as leading man on the Exeter circuit. Some of the two guineas a week he got for this went on drink—it was not unknown, even in these early days, for him to be too incapable to perform—some went to help keep a distressed and unhappy young wife and two children. This sad quartet had known what it was to tramp the roads begging and barn-storming; and the father had known what it was to have to sell their pitiful belongings for need of food. 'Today I must dine' he said on the day he went to face his first London audience. His fellow actors were unsympathetic; the young actor had revealed heretical innovations at his one rehearsal at twelve that morning. The theatre was only a quarter full.

Shylock shook the house out of its lethargy. 'How the devil so few of them kicked up such a row' said a fellow actor 'was something marvellous.' Kean dashed home. 'Mary, you shall ride in your carriage, and Charley shall go to Eton.' Only two critics had attended but Hazlitt was one of them, and he spoke out in such favourable terms of this and later performances that Kean's success gradually became assured. 'His books show a sum nearly averaging £10,000 a year for eighteen years . . . yet a few days before his death he was in danger of an arrest for a sum not exceeding £100.' He died in his middle forties, burnt out by excesses both of genius and indulgence, with a claim to immortality and barely a penny to his name. But Charley had gone to Eton.

Anarchy's dark child, Kean's irregular genius split the town. The purists would hear no good of the 'little ill-looking vagabond', the 'pot-house actor' with the 'low and meagre figure' and hoarse voice 'somewhat between an apoplexy and a cold' who, strongly fortified by brandy, so passionately defaced the stage's monuments of conformity—and no less passionately flaunted all social conventions. The romantic radicals would hear no ill. 'Life, nature, truth, without exaggeration or diminution' said Byron of his Richard III. 'Like a chapter of Genesis' said Douglas Jerrold of his Shylock. Less literary but equally compelling is Leveson Gower's letter about Othello: 'I never saw such acting. I am not sure whether I like it; admire it I must—it is nature. Should tragedy be quite so natural? There wants a spice of Dignity; the passions would be disgusting were they represented so exact . . . I was frightened, alarmed; I cannot account for what I felt. I wished to be away, and saw those eyes all night and hear "Damn her! Damn her!" still—it was too horrible.' Fanny Kemble, Siddon's niece, and herself an actress of distinction, though she had 'lived among those whose theatrical creed would not permit them to acknowledge him as a great actor' grants him genius and her measured, temperate judgement comes graciously from a new generation. 'Kean possesses particular physical qualifications: an eye like an orb of light, a voice exquisitely touching and melodious in its tenderness, and in the harsh dissonance of vehement passion terribly true: to these he adds the intellectual ones of vigour, intensity, amazing power of concentrating effect—these give him an entire mastery over his audience in all striking, sudden, impassioned passages, in fulfilling which he has contented himself, leaving unheeded what he could not compass—the unity of conception, the refinement of detail, and evenness of execution. If he was irregular and unartistlike in his performance, so is Niagara compared with the waterworks of Versailles.'

We may guess that Kean's strength lay in his energetic villains. He chose first to be seen as Shylock and Richard and we may be sure that he himself knew that these would show him to best advantage. His best things in Hamlet, all the passages of vehemence, Hazlitt thought 'in a higher cast of excellence than any part of his Richard' but found him too virulent in much of the character, too much of the actor and not enough of the Prince. His Othello could be expected to score, despite his lack of inches, in all the scenes of primitive violence but 'he is too often in the highest key of passion, too uniformly on the verge of extravagance, too constantly on the rack'. What must have come as unexpected was 'the tone of voice in which he delivered the beautiful apostrophe, 'Then, oh, fare-well!' which struck on the heart like the swelling notes of some divine music, like the sound of years of departed happiness. Why not all so, or all that is like it?' So decisive an actor as Kean no doubt missed much of the poetry of indecision in *Macbeth* but Hazlitt found the scene after the murder one of his two greatest—'as a lesson in humanity, it was heartrending. The hesitation, the bewildered look, the coming to himself when he sees his hands bloody; the manner in which his voice clung to his throat, and choked his utterance, his agony and tears, the force of nature overcome by passion—beggared description. It was a scene which no one who saw it can ever efface from his recollection'. Despite Hazlitt's 'he was all energy, or nothing' it seems that what Kean did best, he did better than anyone before or since.

Three rivals rose to challenge Kean. He acted with them all and demolished them all. A few years after Kean's initial success, Lucius Junius Brutus Booth created something of a stir playing Kean's parts in the Kean manner. Kean, all smiles, invited Booth to play Iago to his own Othello and made such rings round him that, when it came to the second encounter, Lucius Junius (literally) ran away and hid. Young was a much more serious rival. Though he was in the classic Kemble mould, Kean himself thought him a good actor—'with his personal advantages and his damn musical voice'. They played a whole season together in 1822 and Kean had to call up all his reserves of finesse to bolster a fading energy, and cunningly choose parts that would favour him in the comparison. It was eleven years before he took part in any further such competitions. He was half dead, 'tarnished metal', when he was seen with Macready. Crippled with gout, his voice all but gone, Kean resolutely upstaged his gentlemanly rival and was able to throw in just enough flashes of his old fire to make sure that all could see how chill was his opponent. Kean knew one more Iago—though no rival—his son Charles. Half way through the performance he fell, insensible and dying, into his son's arms and was borne off, never to return. Two months later, in his middle forties, he was dead.

Kemble had been statuesque and Olympian; Kean was fiery and elemental; Macready, introspective and intelligent, conscientiously laboured in pursuit of excellence. Kean had flashed the intermittent lightning of his genius onto isolated moments of horrific beauty. Macready, earnestly and worthily, held up his little candle's even light to a correctly balanced reading of a whole part. He might be correct where Kean was vulgar, and reliable where Kean was erratic, but he had neither Kean's magic nor Kemble's majesty. His best talents were for the domestic in drama and he might have fared more comfortably (if no better) had the revolution to realism in play-writing come earlier.

The State of the Theatres

London At the close of the eighteenth century, at least seven minor theatres were providing competition to the theoretical monopoly of the two patent theatres. 'Musical' plays were held not to infringe the monopoly and a few pieces of incidental music and the addition of not less than six songs sufficed to permit performances of almost any play from *King Lear* to *The Beaux' Stratagem*. In 1843 the Act for Regulating the Theatres removed the cramping monopoly, thus permitting new theatres to be built and new plays to be written without recourse to the artificial 'musical' additions. The showmen who ran the small irregular theatres had, however, been forced by the old monopoly to learn many new tricks to attract custom. These had proved so popular, and had such an enduring influence, that it was many years before the legitimate drama could shake off the shackles.

Stage Lighting In 1817 gas lighting replaced the old candles and lamps. A considerable increase in the strength of light was provided by this means and by the middle of the century a new flexibility was made possible by the prompter's manipulation of the gastable, or control, which could vary the output of each individual light. As late as the 1890s, however, sensible complaints were being made of the uniform glare of stage lighting: 'There are no shadows . . . you cannot see the face for the light.' Not until the end of the century, when Irving darkened the auditorium and began to use lighting with something of the artistry of a painter, was the new medium mastered. At which point electricity arrived.

Provincial Theatres The era of great acting that spanned from Garrick's arrival in 1741 to Macready's retirement in 1851 owed much, particularly during its middle and later period, to the invaluable training ground that the provinces provided for actors in their period of apprenticeship. Kemble and Jordan had both come from York, Siddons from Bath; and Garrick and Woffington had found it profitable to visit Dublin. Bath had a theatre in 1705, one of the earliest, and was soon followed by Bristol (1729), York (1734) and Ipswich (1736). Norwich had joined them by the middle of the century and Hull, Liverpool, Manchester and Newcastle were established by 1788 when an Act was passed legalizing acting in the provinces. From each centre, the actors toured a circuit of lesser towns in the area. The York circuit, for example, had six theatres by 1805 and the East Anglian circuit eleven by 1828. In the 1790s stars were brought from London to head the resident provincial companies for a week or two, and this was found so successful that the custom increased.

Strolling Players Lesser actors in small groups travelled the smaller towns and villages playing in barns and booths with only as much scenery and costumes as they could carry on their wagon—or even, in the case of the very poor ones, on their backs. Siddons herself, in her youth, had seen service among the strollers. And, in the early years of the new century, Kean, in his teens, followed the same desperate roads.

Popular Theatre—Early Melodrama

> "I am thy father"
> "Behold thy mother"
> "Your sister is dumb"
> "Your brother is an idiot"
> "I swear to be thine"
> "The enemy is British and will die or conquer"
> "Should the enemy prove victorious blow up the ship"

The words were not spoken but writ large and bold on scrolls and displayed to the audience—also to relevant characters in the play who, if the action could not be made clear in any other way, replied with a further scroll. The law said that only at Covent Garden and Drury Lane might characters in a play speak aloud to each other, and the two patent

Provincial theatre—Bristol   Built in 1766, the present-day theatre retains most of its original features—more than any other theatre extant in this country. (*Photo by Desmond Tripp*)

Melodrama

THE HEROINE IN TROUBLE AGAIN. Louisa, in *London by Night*, 1844, takes the only way out. (*Author's collection*)

Anti-hero by Cruikshank

Anti-villain by Cruikshank. (*Author's collection*)

theatres zealously attacked any of the minor theatres that threatened their monopoly. Hence the placard sentiments. Hence the whole heterogeneous medley of early melodrama. It was the popular theatre's gesture to tragedy, as pantomime had earlier been to comedy.

Denied dialogue, the characters had to act out their stories in dumb show. Cut out a character's tongue and you cut out his complexity. The visual shorthand of a fair face quickly came to signal the hero, a black beard the villain—and, surely, a skirt could hide nothing but virtue? The conditions predetermined a simplicity of approach; and, anyway, that was the way simple people liked it. The prattle gone, it was necessary to magnify and elaborate the action. Variety and attraction were lent to the performance by ample helpings of singing, dancing, combats, pageantry and all the increasing resources of the scenic department. And if men might not talk, monkeys could be made to chatter, dogs to bark, horses to snort, and whole menageries to run through their lively gamut. It is the time of the Thespian Horse, the Canine Roscius and the Hippodramatic Theatre, when a proud manager could boast of his good fortune in being able to engage the 'superior strength' of Burmah bulls, elephants and ostriches. The managers literally cut the cackle and came to the hosses. And dramatic critics dexterously enlarged their frontiers to include praise for acting horses who fought and died, 'climbed up walls perpendicular, or scampered longitudinally, and leaped through breaches with the greatest ingenuity' and to find superlatives for the star of the troupe, when he 'knelt, he leaped, he tumbled, he danced, he fought, he dashed into water and up precipices in a very superior style of acting'. This was in 1811—not for nothing had Billy, the Little Military Learned Horse, struggled to lay down the traditions of his craft way back in 1768. When told by his master, Astley, that he must go to fight the Spaniards, this Garrick among horses, gave a lifelike performance of an old soldier feigning lameness, sickness, a headache, and finally shammed dead; until, ordered to fight the Germans, he leapt ardently to his feet and fired a pistol. Monkeys were early in the field. 1753 found them among Mrs Midnight's Animal Comedians, beseiged in a smoking fortress, repulsing and throwing from the battlements and scaling ladders, hordes of cocky little dogs, trim in coats, tricorne hats and tie-wigs. In 1816 Dog Bruin drew the crowds to Sadler's Wells to witness his two great scenes in the great Aquatic Drama *Philip and His Dog*. First he rescued an infant child from the foaming torrent (real water) where the villain had thrown it; then, in the great final scene when the villain, hotly pursued, threw himself off the cliff and plunged into the waters of the great tank (90ft. by 23ft.), he was promptly followed by the Canine Roscius who, quick as a flash, seized him by the throat and drowned him. Dog Bruin was no innovator —he, too, had a long and distinguished tradition to follow. Back in 1783 Moustache and thirteen other talented dogs, recruited from the fairs of Leipzig and Frankfurt, had given an unforgettable performance in a play which held the stage (as nothing had ever done before) for a whole season's uninterrupted run and netted the lucky manager of Sadler's Wells a clear £10,000 profit. Like Mrs Mountain's dogs, thirty years before, Moustache and his colleagues enacted soldiers storming a fort but, when one of them feigned to run away, he was made to face a firing squad. Dibdin wrote the play and it was called *The Deserter*. It is still performed, in one version or another, in circuses all over the world.

117

When, in 1789, the French Revolution came and the Bastille was stormed, it was a heyday for the stage carpenters. Night after night they hauled down the detachable blocks of the stage Bastille to roars of applause. Nelson's victories, the Siege of Gibraltar and the Battle of the Nile, played right into the hands of the Aquatic Drama. At Sadler's Wells, the Nautical Drama and the Patriotic Drama combined in 'presenting that memorable monument of British Glory, the Siege of Gibraltar . . . with real Men of War (about three feet long) and Floating Batteries, built and rigged by professional men from His Majesty's Dock Yards, and which float in a receptacle containing nearly eight thousand cubic feet of real water . . . the ships firing their broadsides, the conflagration of the town in various places, the defence of the garrison, and attack by the floating batteries, is so faithfully and naturally presented, that when the floating batteries take fire, some blowing up with a dreadful explosion, and others, after burning to the water's edge, sink to the bottom; while the gallant Sir Roger Curtis appears in his boat to save the drowning Spaniards, the British tars for that purpose plunging into the water, the effect is such as to produce an unprecedented climax of astonishment and applause'. The nobility and gentry flocked to join the Well's riff-raff audience, and Jolly Jack Tars became a staple ingredient in melo-drama's stories.

Bleeding nuns, bleeding statues; spectres, ghosts and phantom fiends; devils, vampires, witches and sorceresses; goblins and fairies. To the stories of super-heroes and super-villains was added the extra dimension of the supernatural. The Gothic craze came, the stage delved down into the Dungeon Drama, and the Spectral Legion wailed their

Mrs Midnight's animal comedians 1753
Trained dogs besiege a fort and are repulsed by the monkeys within. (*Author's collection*)

Grimaldi and the Alpaca By *ca.* 1811, most of the changes had been rung on animal performances. Dogs, monkeys, horses (to say nothing of bulls, elephants and ostriches) had run their gamut. Grimaldi, the greatest of our clowns, could not only make the oldest of tricks look new, but was always surprising even those who had come to expect surprises from him, as in this scene from *The Red Dwarf*, Covent Garden

Melodrama at Bartholomew Fair

Cruikshank's coloured engraving gives a fine impression of the sort of performance that delighted audiences in the early nineteenth century, not only in the fairground theatres the length and breadth of the country, but in the major London Theatre as well. (*Author's collection*)

Two Melodramas

(1) THE CRIME AT SYMON'S YAT, 1843 (Surrey Theatre). Mabel: 'You know how I have loved . . . clung to ye, Hubert, aye, as the wild though tender vine clingeth to the sturdier and friendlier branch . . . something whispers me my days are numbered. Ere I cease to breathe I would be your wife. I implore ye, then, grant my request, if not for my sake . . . for the sake of that innocent which ere long will proclaim it's mother's shame to the world . . . ' Hubert: 'Mabel, the time is ill-chosen to urge such a request (aside) Can she know of my intended marriage already? (to Mabel) Urge me further, and my absence shall afford ye an opportunity of raving to the winds.' (*Author's collection*)

120

(2) CURFEWS SHALL NOT RING TONIGHT—The Chertsey Curfew (1842, Surrey Theatre). To save her lover, it is necessary that Blanche Herriot stay the tolling of the curfew. Blanche: 'Horror! they are about to toll the curfew! should the bell once sound, I am lost . . . now, to see if the weak arm of a woman can arrest its fateful tongue. (Bell vibrates slightly.) Its swing increases, and the timbers groan and quiver with the strain (bell begins to swing) I will endeavour with the mad grasp of a drowning creature to seize the iron messenger of death, and check its signal' (she clings to the clapper). Hugh: (the villain, entering) 'What have we here? the haughty Blanche! Lifeless!! (stoops) No . . . She may yet be mine!' (*Author's collection*)

way through ruined castles, gloomy abbeys, dark forests, misty dells and the sad haunted solitude of hermitages. Gloom and Mystery came to eke the blood and the thunder; and no heroine with an eye to fashion could afford not to be immured. 'Romance' was 'a lovely maniac' to such as Monk Lewis, one of the major melodramatists:

> She loathes the sun, or blazing taper's light.
> The moon-beam'd landscape and tempestuous night,
> Alone she loves; and oft, with glimmering lamp,
> Near graves new open'd, or 'midst dungeons damp,
> Drear forests, ruin'd aisles, and haunted towers,
> Forlorn she roves, and raves away the hours! (*The Castle Spectre*)

No less an actress than Siddons bowed to the mood of the times and went wandering in *The Castle of Montval* and the great Kemble could be heard thundering 'Ruffian, hold! Advance thine arm the tithe part of a hair To injure helpless woman, by my soul etc' and 'He that would cut the love that does entwine And link two loving hearts in unison, Maỹ have man's form; but. . . .' (He-whoing was back, perhaps never to be exiled for long.)

Bandits, robbers and smugglers came to brandish poniards, to cross bridges as they exploded into orderly fragments, and to be entrapped in the final great conflagration as the flames leapt from an old mill's tumbling collapse (the Bastille repainted?) They are the most lovable villains of all, forever lurking in the boskage, flattened under their heavily feathered flower-pot hats, dwarfed by their huge swords, forever drawing one another aside to mutter 'But soft, we are observed'.

When melodrama found a tongue, though it tended now to cut the hosses and come to the cackle, it retained its love of spectacular scenic effects and an insistence on the predominance of lively action over whatever was said. *A Letter to the Dramatists of To-day* (1823) is emphatic in its recommendation, 'Action is the essence of drama; nay its definition: business, bustle, hurly, and combustion dire, are indispensable to effective drama' and goes on to condemn 'poeticity' and plays in which 'action is nothing, and your poetry everything'. But what poeticity it is, how rich the rolling sentences: 'Earth's worst plays were full of Heaven's best sentiments.'* Listen to them as they rave and rant, the villains. . . . 'Many a revolution shall the earth make round the sun ere he beholds a deed to equal mine.' 'He shall hang! hang! hang! and on the same gibbet as myself! And how I will exult, and how my eye-balls, starting from their sockets, will glare upon him in their convulsive brilliancy!' 'Demon as I am . . . the little that remains of heart within this wizard frame sustained by human blood, shrinks from the appalling act. . . . Margaret! Unhappy maid! . . . thy blood must feed a Vampire's life, and prove the food of his disgusting banquet.' 'We all have our faults.' 'Aha, I must throw them off their guard by my urbanity,' 'Foil'd at last! And by a woman!' All opponents were not all villainy: 'He is wounded and a prisoner, therefore no more an enemy—take this cross, I bear a few about

---

* The phrase is Willson Disher's. His two books *Blood and Thunder* and *Melodrama* should be compulsory reading (and a great delight) for all who feel themselves drawn to the subject.

me.' Providence was never supposed to sleep over innocence distressed; but always nodded off, tactfully, for long enough to permit the heroine to encounter (and reject) countless fates worse than death. 'To quit the roof of a parent is the most alarming indiscretion of which a female can be guilty; she forfeits the regard of the author of her being; and is thus too apt to supply the loss by accepting a protection which brings with it dishonour and ruin.' 'There does not exist a greater wretch than he, who, by persuasion and perjury, seduces to shame the object of his passion.' (Hereabouts the villain mutters 'This grows wearisome'.) It is hard to know which of the hero's moods is more beguiling, the jauncy 'I did not know I had so much pluck' or the full-throttled 'I trust the day is not so far distant, when so foul a stain to our national character as the laceration of a fellow-creature's flesh, will be blotted from old England's naval and military code for ever'.

In time the melodrama lost its innocence and got embroiled in domesticity, involved in human problems almost probable. Thus, wedded to near–reality, it lost much of its virgin charm. This, fortunately, is enshrined for ever (I hope) among the Penny Plain, Twopence Coloured sheets of the Juvenile Toy Theatre, which can still be bought (with a book of words)—and treasured.

Mid-Century

> Thine it is that the drama did not die,
> Nor flicker down to brainless pantomime
> And those gilt-gauds men-children swarm to see.

Thus Tennyson paid tribute to Macready 'moral, grave, sublime'. Time has not been as

'Uneasy Sits the Head'

Macready, 'Moral, grave, sublime' as Richard III —a detail from a twopenny coloured print published by Hodgson in 1822. (*Author's collection*)

123

kind as Tennyson in its judgement of the kind of new plays with which Macready was associated. 'Gilt-gaud' will do very nicely for Lytton's *Lady of Lyons* and *Richelieu*; and if *Money* is less gaudy, it rings with no great truth. Many have seen it as revolutionarily realistic, a stepping-stone on to the truer drama that was to come. It now seems little more than melodrama in evening dress and starched dicky, its satire crude, and its major characters quite as incredible as any in the more honest Transpontine Drama of the Twopenny Coloureds—you might call it a Sixpenny Plain. It is not till the sixties that any dramatist of marked interest arrives, and we have to wait till the end of the century for a major dramatist.

Shakespeare Restored *King Lear* without the Fool. *King Lear* with a love-interest added for Cordelia and Edgar. Siddons in *Coriolanus* pounding out a Volumnia only half Shakespeare's, the other half thudding fustian by Thomson. Kean hauled over the coals by *The Times* for rejecting this hodge-podge version in favour of a more predominantly Shakespearean text. Coleridge, Lamb, Hazlitt and Leigh Hunt, the leading critics, hammering away at the managers to reform the debased texts. Benedick in *Much Ado About Nothing* jesting through sunlit Messina in the full uniform of a British Infantry Officer of 1810, accompanied by a Leonato in the dress of an English Gentleman of the year 1750. Kemble as Richard III fighting the Battle of Bosworth in spotless silk stockings and dancing shoes, or rushing into Lear's madness and Macbeth's murders in a Louis XV flowered satin night-gown. Kemble as Coriolanus in a costume magnificently correct 'even to his sword' though 'those of his guards had served the heroes of other times and nations' and treading the streets of a Rome that gave 'a pretty exact representation of Hanover-Square, and some very neat Bond-Street shops'.

From Kemble to Macready this was the order of the day. Though Macready and others made isolated and gallant attempts to restore a purer text, though Planché dressed Charles Kemble's *King John* in 1824 in exact Habits of the Period and followed the success of this with similar treatments of *Henry IV* and *Cymbeline*, these were revolutionary steps rather than normal custom. What they did was to pave the way for two very different men who would extend the reformations in two very different ways, one laudable and one laughable. Phelps, for something like eighteen years, gave London the nearest thing to a National Theatre that it had yet known (or was to know for a long time to come). Charles, the great Kean's son, spent thousands of pounds where Phelps spent hundreds—but to less purpose.

Charles Kean's productions of Shakespeare at the Princess's Theatre from 1852 to 1859 suffered from what Peter Ustinov, speaking of similar vulgarities in our own day, has aptly diagnosed as Veneer Disease. Ragamuffin Kean had sent his son Charles to Eton and it was as a scholar that the latter sought to impress, 'to convey information to the general public through the medium of refined amusement'. His audience, like captive schoolchildren, were bombarded with scholarship; his interminable programme-notes were even heavier than his scenery. Correctness, as he saw it, was all. Unfortunately, the standards by which he satisfied himself were more archaeo-logical than logical. Your playbill for *The Winter's Tale* might tell you that 'the cornice on which the roof rests is sup-

Charles Kean's 'The
Winter's Tale',
Princess' Theatre
1836

This illustration of Hermione's trial (from the *Illustrated Times*) typifies the grandiose staging
by which the younger Kean subdued the mere play to opportunities for pageantry and spectacle.
(*Author's collection*)

Charles Kean's
'The Tempest'

Princess' Theatre 1857—Prospero speaks the Epilogue. What Shakespeare allows as but a
moment in the play, is seized on by Kean as an opportunity for an extravagant tableau.
(*Author's collection*)

A **conveyor** of 'Information to the General Public through the Medium of Refined Amusement'. Charles Kean, as Manager, sits beneath the portrait of C. Kean as Hamlet—a detail from a caricature in which he is seen overpaying an author who also happens to be Dramatic Critic to *The Times*. (*Author's collection*)

THE BRITISH

THEATRE

ported by Canephorae'; but it wouldn't tell you why Autolycus, the Clown and the Shepherd had their speeches cut to shreds. Your play-bill for *A Midsummer Night's Dream* might tell you why Charles had rejected the archaeologically correct buildings 'rude in construction' for the more tempting view of Athens at a later period (Ruins Restored Here) which included the summit of Mars Hill and 'on the hill of the Acropolis, the far-famed Parthenon, the Erechtheum, and the statue of the tutelary goddess Minerva, or Athena; by its side the theatre of Bacchus in advance, the temple of Jupiter Olympus, partially hiding the hall of the Museum; and on the right, the temple of Theseus'. But it wouldn't tell you why he could boast that the play was given 'with the original text' when the first scene, to take only one example, lost the irreplaceable beauty of one hundred of its two hundred and fifty lines. Or why Puck's first speeches are given to a fairy so that the nine-year-old Miss Ellen Terry's sprite might rise to music on a mechanical mushroom. In short, in eight years ten plays received massive maltreatment, their texts cut to the bone to permit time for the erection and dismantling of an abundance of edifices 'restored from contemporaneous buildings, in the absence of absolute vestiges'. Had we been there, of what should we have been thinking, during the long, long waits while the stage carpenters

126

struggled and the great unwieldy hunks of solid scenery went laboriously rumbling and trundling? That we had come to hear Shakespeare and been fobbed off with 'gilt-gauds'? Surely that we should have done better to take our glutted eyes and starved ears on that troublesome journey out to Sadler's Wells and find out what the gallant Phelps was doing.

Samuel Phelps Phelps, at the age of thirty-three, and fresh from provincial triumphs had been engaged by Macready for his Covent Garden season of 1837, but proved so successful a rival in his early performances that Macready hurriedly reduced him to second-rate parts. 'I was kept back by Young and Kean, and you will have to wait for me.' Phelps was no match for Macready in these jungle tactics and, although he made a strong impression on the rare occasions when he was given anything like an opportunity, it was not until he became a manager himself that he really made his mark. When the Act of 1843, largely as a result of Macready's strenuous and admirable advocacy, revoked the exclusive monopoly of the two patent theatres, the Shakespeare plays and the other 'regular' drama were now free to all to produce where they liked. What had been for years the home of Aquatic Melodrama and the haunt of dissolute riff-raff became a respected and respectable national theatre. 'Eddystone Elf' with its lighthouse and demon cave went up in flames and Shakespeare and his poetry took over. Phelps was in charge at Sadler's Wells for eighteen years; and he made of those years a landmark in the history of our theatre.

Thirty-four of Shakespeare's plays (that is, all but four of them) were performed. Four nights out of every six, Shakespeare was in the programme. Not only the popular plays were given but many that had not been seen in living memory. Moreover, except in very rare instances, they were performed with a proper regard to textual accuracy. Phelps's *Macbeth*, for instance, broke with the tradition of a hundred years whereby the Witches, backed by a full chorus, sang their curses; and abandoned the culinary refinements of an 'improved' text that gloried in such lines as 'Here's juice of toad and oil of adder; These will make the charm grow madder'. Through the ages, few of Shakespeare's plays have undergone such mangling as *A Midsummer Night's Dream*. Garrick, it will be remembered, had added twenty-five songs to Shakespeare's three. Reynolds in 1816 had exceeded even his normal standards of 'improvement' by converting it, at enormous expense to the text, into an opera which did not hesitate to interpolate such flat-footed 'cues for song' as Theseus's 'And since ourselves, we boast not of the pow'r To welcome them in aught, save the plain Rough language of a soldier, Hermia, stand forth, and with thy dulcet tones, Give, give to all, harmonious greetings'. Moreover, he omitted the last scene of the fairies and included in his final tableau—the talk of its day—'the Cretans, the Amazons, the Centaurs, the Minotaur, Ariadne in the Labyrinth, the Mysterious Peplum or Veil of Minerva, the Ship Argo and the Golden Fleece'. Hazlitt (literally) cried 'murder' and spoke of a delightful poem converted into a dull pantomime in which all that was fine in the play was lost to scene-shifters, dressmakers and fiddlers. Reference has already been made to Charles Kean's crippling treatment of the play when he produced it three years after Phelps had shown the right way; but, since it reflects the taste of the times, this is perhaps the moment to record that Charles's pantomime nonsense set up a new long-run record of one hundred and fifty performances. This is the climate in which to examine

Phelps as Cardinal Wolsey, from a painting, now in the Garrick Club, by the actor Forbes-Robertson. (*Courtesy of Garrick Club*)

Phelps's triumph in an age so debased that verisimilitude looked revolutionary. Not only did his presentation of *A Midsummer Night's Dream* vastly exceed in total effect any production of any one of Shakespeare's plays since the dramatist's own hand was over them but—more remarkable—descriptions of it tempt one to the conclusion that it may not have been bettered since.

Victorian critics, alas, are not of the stature of Hazlitt but something of the magic that Phelps contrived emerges firmly from what is available. By 1853 Phelps had enjoyed nine years of experience in his own theatre and was at his zenith. He had learned to trust his author and his text of the play was without interpolations and substantially complete. It is not a rich period for actors but it has to be said that undoubtedly there were a number of better performers in London than were to be found in Phelps's company. But the main body of them had been with him a long time and, under his guidance, there was certainly no better ensemble playing. They performed in one style and each production was one man's aim at a total effect as distinct from the competitive histrionics that typified the ill-directed (or un-directed) efforts of the other theatres. What Phelps and his loyal players made of *The Dream* was governed primarily by one single factor, simple in itself—but which, if overlooked (and it constantly is) dooms any production of the play to failure. They made of the play a poem about a dream.

'Mr Phelps has never for a minute lost sight of the main idea. . . . He knew that he was to present mere shadows; that spectators, as Puck reminds them in the epilogue, are to think they have slumbered in their seats, and what appeared before them have been visions. Everything has been subdued at Sadler's Wells to this ruling idea. The scenery is very

128

beautiful, but wholly free from the meretricious glitter now in favour; it is not so remarkable for costliness as for the pure taste in which it and all the stage arrangements have been planned. There is no ordinary scene-shifting; but, as in dreams, one scene is made to glide insensibly into another . . . over all the fairy portion of the play there is a haze thrown . . . its influence is everywhere felt; it subdues the flesh and blood of the actors into something more nearly resembling dream-figures.' Thus Henry Morley; and Douglas Jerrold confirms a similar impression. 'There is a misty transparency about the figures that gives them the appearance of flitting shadows. . . . You fancy you can see the moon shining through them. There they dance and whirl, and are puffed about first from one side and then to another, like a cloud of silver dust . . . so artistically are the different changes of moonlight, fog, and sunrise produced, that you imagine you have been wandering through an entire forest, with a fresh prospect meeting you unexpectedly at every turn.' All was done noiselessly as though 'the smallest sound would have broken the spirit of the dream. . . . The fairies, as they glide in and out of the trees and foliage, give you an idea that they have actually stepped out of them . . . and by long residence . . . had become imbued with the colour of them. They were none of your winged, white-muslin fairies with spangles and butterfly wands, but were real, intangible shadowy beings that . . . would infallibly at the first cockrow melt into thin air'. Not all the actors received unqualified praise; but Puck, we notice with relief, is played by a boy; and Phelps himself as Bully Bottom abandoned the accumulated irrelevance of standard comic business and found his own sure way to Shakespeare's character. His admiring critics stress the absence of caricature and buffoonery and praise the elaborate and delicate means by which he found all of the character's absurd humour without once losing its recognizable humanity or for one moment breaking the fragile spell of the dream-world it must inhabit. And what Phelps, as performer and as director of the ensemble, did for this one play, he did for the rest of his huge and admirable repertoire. His success might vary in degree but his aim remained constant.

Besides keeping Shakespeare in a decently unadulterated form before the public for eighteen years, his programme included both the best of the old classic repertoire and some newer plays. Webster's *Duchess of Malfi*, Otway's *Venice Preserv'd*, Massinger's *New Way to Pay Old Debts*, Goldsmith's *She Stoops to Conquer* and Sheridan's *The Rivals* and *The School for Scandal* belong by proper right to any national theatre programme. If revivals of Lytton's plays, for example, seem to us inappropriate, we may be reasonably certain that we should have thought them appropriate at the time.

It is not given to men to rise wholly above the vices of their times and it may well be that vanity as well as expedience led Phelps to place himself rather firmly in the centre of his stage. Equally it is given to few theatre people to rise so far above the level of their times as he did. Not since Shakespeare's own days (if then) had the plays felt the benefit of a co-ordinated ensemble. If the times allowed Phelps to give the plays far greater scenic assistance than they can ever have known before, he must be given also the credit for keeping the new monster within bounds and fitting the scenery to the play instead of the play to the scenery, when all about him (and for generations to follow) lost their heads and played with the new scenic toys to the detriment of 'the mere words'.

Despite Phelps's range as an actor—he is second only to Garrick in his powers over both tragedy and comedy—it may be that he is only in the second class as a performer. Strangely enough much less evidence has been assembled about an era only a hundred years old than about any other period in theatrical history—it is a dull period for plays and most histories of the theatre tend to be histories of the drama. Moreover, such of the critical writing as one can unearth with ease is not of the calibre of, say, Hazlitt at the beginning of the century or Shaw at the end. Phelps awaits a competent biographer and scholarship has paid little attention to the birth of ensemble playing under one man's direction. It is clear that this currently accepted custom began not with Granville-Barker in the early twentieth century, but fifty years before with Phelps. A book that set out to prove that Phelps did more to interpret Shakespeare on the stage than any one man before or since, might well have its critics, but the claim is not idly made. Much less than justice has been done to this most exceptional man of the theatre.

Enter Realism What should an audience expect in a theatre? An entertaining game or a slice of life? Undisguised theatricality, the audience never forgetting (never *wishing* to forget) that what they are watching is not life but acting, not caring whether the incidents portrayed are convincing, or even probable, just so long as they are exciting? Or the perfection of the illusion that what is happening on the stage could happen in real life—is, indeed, happening—and that you are not sitting in a theatre amongst coughing neighbours but somehow miraculously part of the fourth wall of a real room watching its real inmates doing real things?

What chance had the theatre of the 1860s of persuading an audience that they were watching a slice of life? What chance was there that the audience even wanted to be so persuaded? *Pure as Driven Snow; or Tempted in Vain*, the title of a melodrama seen at the Britannia, Hoxton in the late sixties, characterizes the popular taste. No hint of real people here, only one-dimensional formal heroine and villain; no hint of real speech, only popular moral sentiments, unhand-me-sirring and he-whoing. *The Engineer; or the Life of George Stephenson* came to the Old Vic in 1863, not to show the life of anybody but to exhibit a sectional view of a tunnel, traversed simultaneously by two separate trains, a startling effect produced at prodigious cost. The play (unaccountably) failed. But it was not long before the same solidly-built locomotives and carriages were incorporated by a more clever dramatist into *The London Arab*, a huge success. (A visiting French manager was so impressed that he bought the trains and had them incorporated into a third play to delight Paris audiences. Then an American bought them and had them shipped off, lock, stock and barrel to New York, where they starred in their fourth play.) England found other railway trains and other dramatists to write scenes for them. Boucicault became the major dramatist of his times because of the unparalleled care he took in the construction of his plays. First he thought up his 'sensation', then made a working scale-model of it, then neatly fitted in characters and a story. In *Rescued* (1879) he showed real mastery of his craft with a superb variation on the railway train theme. A swivel bridge, the whirl of a swiftly approaching train rumbling in the spectators' ears, two women exerting superhuman efforts to work the lever that closes the bridge and only succeeding in the very nick of time. Was there any slice of life that could be as excitingly rewarding as that?

Realism versus sensationalism. (Left) Lady Bancroft as Polly Eccles in Robertson's *Caste*. Jack's portrait for 'Society' shows the new heroine engaged in familiar domestic pursuits. (Right) the final scene of *Caste* shows unexaggerated behaviour in a recognizable homely atmosphere. It is interesting to compare these two incidents with the illustration (below) of the melodrama *Under the Gaslight* (which tells its own story). Both plays belong to the year 1867. (*Lady Bancroft and Caste, Author's collection*)

One dramatist, at least, thought so. Tom Robertson was sitting next to a dramatic critic and one incident in a play so excited him that he turned and exclaimed: 'Oh, that I should have lived to hear that sound in a theatre.' What had happened? 'One of the characters left the stage, through an actual door, which he slammed and closed by a real handle, and the door fastening was distinctly heard to click.' To understand Robertson's excitement we need to remember two things. Firstly, that he was the major exponent of the new kind of writing, the slice of life school. Secondly, we must know what a room on the stage commonly looked like prior to this epoch-making moment. Overhead waved some borders painted to represent the sky; at the back a painted cloth shared by windows, views through windows, panelling, a clock or mirror, two chandeliers, a small table with a bowl of flowers, and two chairs—all painted; the side walls of a room have to be imagined, all that can be seen is a series of stock interior wings each side, parallel to the cloth, and, through the gaps between them, a glimpse of prompters, scene-shifters and actors waiting for their cues. If a 'practical' door was incorporated into the backcloth, it would be of flimsy lath and canvas, and its opening would send the whole back wall swaying and flapping. Moreover, it could only be opened from the outside by a stage-hand; the on-stage actor, anxious to get out, standing meanwhile knocking with patient dignity at the door. In the absence of the stage-hand (not unknown) the trapped actor had to choose between risking a strenuous tussle or a haughty exit through the side wall. When the scene came to be changed, the prompter's whistle blew and a table moved off at one side and sofa and chairs at the other—apparently of their own volition. Whatever furniture was needed for the next scene came sliding on equally mysteriously in full view of the audience (as were the cords that drew them and the men in the wings pulling them). Or 'two men running violently towards each other, with half a castle or a garden in their grasp'. It may be seen that that clicking door (with a *real* knob) was revolutionary; but Robertson was concerned with other novel realities, too.

'Oh, unutterable bliss! 'Tis she! She who first conquered my soul, ravished my heart-strings, and put me whole being in a flutter when I first saw her at Milady Nebworthy's tea party t'other noon.' The splendid fellow is bawling this out in a transport of excitement. But, because he is 'speaking aside', the poor girl is not supposed to hear it and has to stand patiently twiddling her parasol and looking demurely but firmly down at her feet until it's her turn, when she will greet him with unfluttered surprise. Legions of lads and lasses had been carrying on like this for years when Robertson's heroine came on the scene. 'I would have existence all like Tennyson' she says but adds 'instead of which it's nothing but butcher's bills.'

Robertson's people, then, spoke like real people and inhabited recognizable, convincingly realistic rooms. Individual characters replaced stock types. The Bancrofts, under whose management at the Prince of Wales Theatre Robertson's plays were presented, had established a reputation for realistic ensemble playing. Robertson was just the author they were looking for; they gave him his head and allowed him to direct his own plays. This he did with a firm hand that determined that performance should substantially reflect the author's intentions. Boucicault had shown what such discipline could do for the melodrama; Robertson showed what it could do for the subtler and more detailed domestic drama. The advantages of disciplined group acting over the old anarchic dog-bite-dog scrambles were so impressive that they led to a tradition of author-directors from which the theatre greatly benefited.

The 'cup-and-saucer' drama, as it was called, had arrived. It was greatly taken up. Not to be outdone by a mere real doorknob, Charles Reade, in 1874, introduced into *Rachel the Reaper* 'real pigs, real sheep, a real goat and a real dog' with 'real litter . . . strewn over the stage'. But more and more of Robertson's successors came, in time, to concentrate on more complex realities—though not to such an extent that any very warm welcome was waiting for Ibsen when he went one better and introduced *real* realities. No chapter in the long history of critical protest is quite so rich in yowls and screeching as that which greeted the first major dramatist of modern times.

Prelude to the Nineties The 1890s were a major turning-point in the history of our theatre. Many reforms only begun in the period do not, of course, come to fruition until much later; just as many threads of reform reach back into earlier times. Nevertheless, since the nineties saw so much that was new locked in such desperate combat with so much that was old, it is here that a dividing-line belongs—and here that a gathering together of causes is proper before we study the effect.

London, by the nineties, had grown from a population of a mere 865,000 in 1801 to become an enormous metropolis linked to a sprawl of new suburbs by extensive rail and road services. A vast new potential audience had access to the sixty-one theatres that served the new London—thirty-eight theatres in the West End and twenty-three in the suburbs. Subject only to the censor, these theatres were free to choose their own programmes; whereas at the beginning of the century a legal monopoly had limited such choice to only two theatres and left half-a-dozen others to operate intermittently and illegally. In the early part of the century it was an ill-bred and riotous audience, the lowest common denominator in taste, that dictated the choice of programme nine nights out of ten; and the theatre was so much the 'haunt of dissolute and depraved persons' that no self-respecting family dared to be seen there. By the end of the period even the most socially timid were safe to attend and a wide variety of plays catered for an increasing range of tastes. Moreover, the audience was not only immeasurably larger in quantity, but with the growth of education, immeasurably higher in quality. (A middle class that had only just taken to reading at the beginning of the century, by the end had turned into a middle class in grave danger of having read too much.)

Within the theatres, too, drastic changes had taken place. Many of the new theatres had a more appropriately intimate atmosphere; most of the actual stages had crept discreetly behind a proscenium that framed the picture of stories that could court the illusion of a photographic likeness to reality. This picture frame divided audience and players but at the same time gave the players an authority over their audience never possible before, an authority strengthened when the new controls over lighting made it possible to darken the auditorium and leave the stage commandingly lit. Advances in scenic and lighting techniques made possible a greater realism in settings and this was furthered with the introduction of the long-run system. A play could now have its own scenery instead of sharing

Disorder turns to decorum

Audience behaviour is well illustrated by these contrasting prints. Above, a Cruikshank engraving (1808) entitled *John Grouse and Mother Goose* shows the actor struggling against the disorder common in the nineteenth century in the theatres—'the haunt of dissolute and depraved persons'. Below, the same theatre, Covent Garden, in the mid-nineteenth century, graced by a royal visit and with full decorum prevailing. (*Author's collection*)

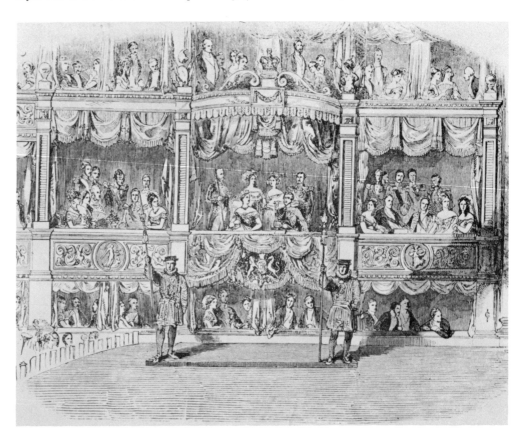

**Charles Dickens in
a public reading,**
from a painting by
Alfred Bryan

*Nineteenth
Century
Theatre*

The enigma of Dickens the Dramatist. From Sheridan in the 1770s until Wilde
in the 1890s—120 years passed during which no major British dramatist emerged. The boy
Dickens was enamoured of acting, began writing when he was 21, wrote two or three plays
when he was 24 (*The Strange Gentleman* ran for seventy nights, a mild success) and spent
much of his adult life either acting as an amateur or giving highly dramatic public readings
of his works. Why did he not become the major dramatist the theatre was needing so badly?
His characters cry out for performance; and he was familiar with stage technique—and could,
with patience, have mastered it. Part of the answer is that the theatre was 'old hat', and the
new popular novels 'all the go'; part that the theatres came to be his enemies, plundering
his works to make plays of his stories even before they were finished. Copyright laws were
slight and ineffectual—he got not a penny from the legion of stage successes plagiarized from
his work. (Many of the amateur performances he gave up and down the country were in
favour of needy writers—Leigh Hunt among them—and he gave much time and energy to
the task of provoking proper copyright laws.) The question remains, at best only partially
answered—Why did Dickens not become a major dramatist? Why did no major actor or
manager take sufficient pains to encourage him to this end?

Contemporary Adaptations to the stage of Dickens' stories
(1) Sam Weller, (2) Oliver Twist, (3) Bleak House, (4) Nicholas Nickleby. (*Author's collection*)

inappropriate pieces from stock. And if the setting was to stand for a long time, it could be given a convincing solidity and a detailed wealth of trimmings.

No theatre can succeed, however, unless it offers an attractive proposition to its dramatists. Copyright acts had been fought for and won, giving authors safeguards over their property which, if not yet fully protective, were at least a substantial hindrance to pirates. The mid-century dramatist was perforce a hack-writer, snatching his stories from Dickens, from Scott, from the French, from all over the Continent, bundling them into manuscript all anyhow, and quickly on to the next, in case hack-writer No. 2 should steal it before he did. He was a slave to conformity, attempting only what had succeeded before—and, above all, a slave to the lowest tastes in his audience. Advances in ensemble-playing in a co-ordinated production under the discipline of a director allowed new authors to believe that what they had dreamed in manuscript might now be realized by the actors who had hitherto rejected anything that, in their very conservative opinion, might not 'go'. The new long runs, and the subsequent new provincial tours, opened up vistas of hitherto unparalleled financial encouragement to potential dramatists.

The ground was laid for an entirely new kind of dramatist—a man who would write a play for little other reason than that it seemed to him the best way to say something that he thought badly needed saying. There were many people aware that society needed reforming; a social reformer could now see the stage as a proper medium for popularizing his theories. His plays would only be seen, at first, by a limited audience at the new matinées when such worthy (but financially risky) ventures might be tried out. But the time was not so very far off when a theatre would be able to devote its entire programme to plays that, if they continued to hold up the mirror to certain aspects of nature, also began to hold up signposts beckoning men away from old hells to new utopias.

Nineteenth Century Theatre

137

'The Naughty Nineties'

Middle-class morality is well illustrated by Toulouse Lautrec in this 1893 litho of two spectators in a box. (The faces repay close study)

The Can-Can, by Toulouse Lautrec. This litho poster of Jane Avril (1893) illustrates superbly the Naughty Nineties atmosphere. (Again the face of this devotee of gaiety repays close study)

CHAPTER EIGHT

The Nineties

The Naughty Nineties they were called and the image that a somewhat arbitrary posterity has bestowed on them is that of a bevy of Toulouse-Lautrec Can-Can dancers energetically hoisting their skirts high above their heads and showing, at last, beautiful bodies that had long lain stifled in protective petticoats. There is, too, an aura of suspicion that the lovely ladies probably lived in intermittent sin, sharing a discreet hide-out in Maida Vale with A Protector—who turned out to be none other than the familiar Victorian father-figure, respectably regarded (if somewhat perplexingly unfulfilled) by his huge family at home. The more clever chorines, it is true, stuck out for a title; but it is pre-eminently the era of Sub Rosa (and what a dear girl Rosa was).

Naughty children are (or were) apt to get smacked. The nineties set out to make their predecessors look childish and gave them one brutal smack in the eye after another. Conformity, half-blinded, reeled like a drunk. And the poor man in the street was perplexed, harassed and heckled by a multitude of moral highwaymen, robin-hooding about all over the place. Disestablishment was established. There was a wild rush to lock up the spoons before the naughty iconoclasts nabbed them for the poor.

Ibsen 'An open drain; a loathsome sore unbandaged; a dirty act done publicly' says the dramatic critic of the *Daily Telegraph*; snatches a breath; then—'absolutely loathsome and fetid. . . . Gross, almost putrid indecorum . . . literary carrion. . . . Crapulous stuff.' The energetic Clement Scott kicks up such a sturdy splash in mid-stream that his colleagues seem to be merely dabbling in the shallows. 'Unutterably offensive . . . naked loathsomeness . . . dismal and repulsive . . . revoltingly suggestive and blasphemous . . . abhorrent . . . repulsive and degrading . . . morbid, unhealthy, unwholesome and disgusting . . . merely dull dirt long drawn out . . . morbid horrors . . . outrage . . . wicked nightmare . . . sor-

139

did . . . garbage and offal . . . foul and filthy.' Having done with the play, they turn to the author—'Egotist . . . bungler . . . crazy fanatic . . . crazy, cranky being . . . pessimist . . . suburban . . . provincial . . . lob-worm symbolist.'

Ibsen had caught them Sub Rosa with their trousers down and hit them where it hurt. This was not playing the game. Society had a bit of a squint at the time, gained from long practice in turning a blind eye to Certain Things. A man of the world was entitled to his 'bit of fun', healthy youngsters must be expected to 'sow their wild oats'—and romantic Rosa was just the girl for the job, the proper maid-of-all-work for Maida Vale. Any man worthy of the name was bound to be driven to do things that were Not Really Done. You could back-slide on some of the Ten Commandments so long as you never broke the sacred eleventh—'Thou shalt not talk about it.' ('Not at home, anyway!')

Ibsen's *Ghosts* pointed out that no such Rose was without thorns; that a man might pass on to his son the marks of her canker; and that then there was not enough champagne in the whole world to wash off the taint of that madness. In short, Rose might land you with V.D. And then all your son would have to look forward to, would be the moment when the general paralysis of insanity destroyed him. The play is not only an exposée of philandering but of a marriage made not for love but for social convenience. It goes even further and questions whether the sacrifice of life to an ideal like marriage is not useless. It faces facts. It was a world of sham to which Ibsen held up the mirror so fair and square. No wonder the critics tried to kick the mirror to pieces. The nineties are a long way off now and there are still many who will face neither the facts, nor the play.

Ghosts was about things that are Not Done; *A Doll's House* lifted the curtain on just such an exemplary household as Ibsen's audience thought they wished themselves to be

The man who frightened them

Ibsen—from a signed photograph given to Mr W. Heinemann

living in. Its model father, mother and children share, it seems, 'The sweet home . . . the happy family life of the idealist's dream' but events force them to see how far human frailty is separated from romantic daydreams. Ibsen pointed out that when you incautiously think of the uneasy partnership between a man and a woman as A Perfect Marriage, you embrace an illusion, court disaster, live with a lie and breed tragedy. Romantic fiction had always ended with the lover's kiss. Ibsen made this the starting point of a much more grown-up story.

A Doll's House was the long-delayed epilogue to the Eighteenth Century's Theatre of Sentiment. Ghosts was the long-shirked sequel to the Restoration's plays of the Gallants. The Wild Duck was a very prompt sequel to the Plays of Reform—so prompt that the near-sighted thought that Ibsen was merely satirizing himself. Into a poor home made to seem rich by romantic illusions comes a reformer, hell-bent on exposing as much of the truth as he can see. The result is stark tragedy for the family and the exposure of a shallow idealist who confuses his romantic desire to meddle with a practical ability to help forward. The tragi-comedy illustrates with dreadful irony the dangers to society of men so gluttonous for reform that they embrace it romantically. It takes more than a wild duck to bring freedom to a tame farmyard.

'Go out from the moral leper-house . . . and tell us something of the cleanliness that is next to Godliness.' So Clement Scott fulminates finely for Ibsen's opponents. Bernard Shaw took up the cudgels for 'the greatest living dramatic poet and moral teacher'. So the anti-Ibsenites called him a 'muck-ferreting dog'. Twenty years later, when Shaw re-issued his earlier primer on Ibsen, brought up to date to include the later plays, he wondered whether Ibsen's work was not facing an even greater danger than abuse: 'The most effective way of shutting our minds against a great man's ideas is to take them for granted and admit he was great and have done with him.' Now, some seventy years later, it seems probable that Ibsen has by no means done with us. Any attempt to dismiss the plays as merely topical or local in their application exposes not the play but the critic. At a time when suffragettes were so strenuously demonstrating for Women's Rights, Ibsen's A Doll's House seemed to be about a wife deprived by a man-made society of the fuller life not to be found in mere petted domesticity. By 1939 James Agate was indicating that this was every bit as much her own fault as her husband's. Subsequent times have found other interpretations. And no doubt the play will be found much in vogue (and look somewhat different yet again) when Society at long last gets round to seriously questioning our present anachronistic attitude to Marriage and The Family as the best and only way of organizing the War and Peace of the sexes and their children. The play, like the other major Ibsen plays, is not a topical tract but a profound and universal study of human relationships. The beauty and validity of the plays is not just skin-deep but organic, in the bones and flowing through the whole structure. Ibsen's critics had been conditioned to a theatre that was like a florist's shop, full of forced blooms. Ibsen's plays have the beauty not of flowers in a vase but of the whole plant—its roots, foliage, flowering and seed-making, its intercourse with sun, rain, wind, with its neighbours, and with the grubby and miraculous fecundity of the earth from which it sprang and which it will enrich for future seeds when it dies.

It is not Ibsen but one of his characters who says: 'All the wisdom of the world consists

141

in being capable of living one's life without ideals.' To take what one character says at one moment in one Ibsen play and advance it as the dramatist's creed for living would be as naïve as to attempt to sum up Shakespeare's philosophy from Hamlet's 'There's a divinity that shapes our ends, rough hew them how we will'. At first sight the two quotations appear to epitomize two extremes of thought. *Examine what happens to the characters who believe these thoughts* and the two dramatists emerge not as distant relations but close cousins. It is not only a depth in philosophy and human awareness that unites them but a mastery of their craft. This is so mighty in Ibsen that it at once places him, technically, as the most complex and rewarding dramatist since the Elizabethan.

In the same way that we have not yet worked out the social problems posed in Ibsen's plays, we have not yet assimilated into our drama their technical lessons. In a short section of a short book, one example must serve. Ibsen revolutionized the handling of a play's exposition; the method is so palpably rewarding that one is amazed that so many present-day dramatists continue to slave away in the old pre-Ibsen manner. You know (too well) the sort of thing. Lord Standworthy's butler, as the curtain rises, tells a telephone what the dramatist thinks the audience needs to know about the household; then two characters come on and tell one another things about each other that they both obviously already know, just because the dramatist thinks that we need to know them before he can get his story started. Ibsen starts his play, as it were, in the middle—without an exposition. What's that woman, is she his wife or his sister, is she a visitor or at home here? We feel at once as if we are invisible spectators in someone else's house and, consumed with curiosity, we start sorting them all out. No sooner have we decided which characters are to have our sympathy (old habits die hard and we're still playing at heroes and villains), when the wife we like so much does something we don't like and the unlikeable husband seems suddenly likeable, you don't know where you are with them, they're just like human beings, what unforeseeable things *will* they be up to next? On the surface everything has been real; under the surface the dramatist has been excelling in an exercise in suspense. When all the outstanding questions that we accumulate in the course of the play are eventually answered, the answers are welcomed by minds made eager because they are involved and concerned.

The pre-Ibsen exposition only states a proposition before we have become involved. It arouses our hostility because of its palpable artifice and makes a wanton waste of time, credibility and proper suspense. This is only one of many technical anachronisms in regular present-day use. Many dramatists, whether serious or popular, are still deploying a whole horde of antiquated technical devices equally inappropriate in the modern theatre; many of these they would not hesitate to jettison if they cared to extend their scope by a thorough investigation of Ibsen's technique. Not with the intent to copy Ibsen but to enlarge their own means by studying his; by putting the plays on the dissecting table and trying to unravel the complex inevitability of every part of them. To ascertain whether or no it is valid that not a word that is said, not an incident that takes place, that does not advance significantly the proper interaction of theme and story and contribute to the justice of their total gesture. To observe how suspense is aptly engendered and how surprise is made appropriate—and yet credibility is never threatened. Never threatened, that is, unless we persist is seeing all houses as bungalows in which we can never be asked to go upstairs. Ibsen sees truth as existing not only in the ground-floor's undertones of reality but in the allegorical overtones that haunt the upper storey. Man is not mere visibly recognizable man but also representative mankind. A play is not a mere social survey but also an evocative poem. Problems need more illumination than can be given by just shining a bright light on them; that may give them a superficial reality—but no *ultimate* credibility. The best thing about Ibsen's plays is not just that they pass with such high honours the test of what seems right in the immediacy of the theatre. That might only be the start of a love affair. We have lived with them some fifty or more years and familiarity has bred respect. Seen in long retrospect, after close familiarity and searching study, the complex patterns seem to have the final justice of unassailable inevitability. The plays are not so much real as true.

The Ibsen plays, when first seen in England, were given only a very limited number of performances, more often than not a mere handful, sometimes only a single special matinée. J. T. Grein offered some of them for a more extended viewing when he established his Independent Theatre but, in these early days, only a very few people saw the plays in a theatre. Thousands of copies of the printed plays were sold, however, and Bernard Shaw kept the topic alive, not only with his book, *The Quintessence of Ibsenism,** but week in week out, in his articles as a dramatic critic. Ibsen was the yardstick against which he measured the more serious dramatists who now began to write with a greater independence on past methods. Shaw also turned a critical eye on the Dependent Theatre. The Lyceum was the very successful citadel of the traditional theatre and Shaw was not going to be blinded to its shortcomings because it was also the home of two players of rare genius— Henry Irving and Ellen Terry.

Henry Irving Irving was a spell-binder. Ibsen and Shaw were spell-breakers. The world of romantic idealism that they sought to expose as unreal and dangerous was the world that Irving (and most of society) still saw as real and comfortable—and a proper play-ground. Irving can only be judged in terms of what had gone before; so much of his genius was alien to what was to come. As an actor he was a true descendant of the great actors of the past; his genius was his own but yet held echoes of Kean's lightning, Kemble's grandeur, Garrick's versatility and Macready's serious intellectual self-concentration. He chose his plays as Macready had done, a programme strangely mingling Shakespeare and near-Shakespeare (Tennyson's and the other verse plays are not many stages removed from Lytton's) with a liberal dash of trusty melodramas. He directed his plays in a manner evolved from that which Charles Kean had popularized, the Shakespeare texts maltreated to permit sumptuous scenery—why had he learnt nothing from Phelps? His company were well-drilled to sustain their characters in a theatrically effective manner and not to hog the star's limelight—why had he learnt nothing from the Bancrofts and their ensemble playing? Perhaps it is a waste of time to ponder what he did not do, when so much that he did was so fine. If a magician offered us the choice of being present at the first English performance of *Ghosts* or watching Irving in *The Bells*, should we not plead to see both?

'In quest of bustling romances or melodramas he seemed generally to alight on hack-

* I wonder how many others find the title as forbidding as I do. For years, though I was an avid Shavian, it kept me from a book I now regard as required reading for anyone interested in Ibsen, twentieth century theatre or social philosophy. Not only required reading but a stimulating pleasure.

Above, **A caricature of Irving** between England and America, 1883, by Cee Bee after Sir Joshua Reynolds

Below, **Garrick between comedy and tragedy**—the Reynolds picture which prompted the Irving Caricature above. (*Author's collection*)

Hamlet Caricature by A. B. from *Sporting and Dramatic*, 1892

Irving the spell-binder—as Mephistopheles in *Faust* from a drawing by Bernard Partridge in the *Illustrated London News*. (*Copyright Illustrated London News*)

Othello in a Passion, caricature, 1876. (*Author's collection*)

work. I think there can be no doubt that he was lacking in literary sense.' But Max Beerbohm praises Irving as the first man to give Shakespeare 'a setting that should match the pleasure of the eye with the pleasure of the ear. . . . Irving may have sometimes overdone it; but he always overdid it beautifully'. Praise for anything visual from so fastidious a critic must be put in the balance against our guesses at a vulgar opulence. Irving was so much a man of the romantic theatre, Shaw has so spiritedly attacked him for a lack of intellect, and so much the majority of his praises have been sung in romantic terms, that it comes as something of a surprise to find that we have to query to what extent he was a romantic actor. 'He could not, even had the stage been as bare as a desert, have given us the true music and magic of Shakespeare's verse. He could not declaim.' He was quite unlike the rough-and-ready, orotund fellows who, said Beerbohm, plunged magnificently but without a thought in their heads. 'They had no pretensions to intellect. Irving had . . . and he never failed to justify them. One missed the music of the verse, but was always arrested, stimulated, by the meanings that he made the verse yield to him. These subtle and sometimes profound meanings were not always Shakespeare's own. Now and again, the verse seemed to yield them to Irving only after an intense effort, and with rather a bad grace.'

'His voice, face, figure, port, were not transformable. But so fine was the personality to which they belonged that none cried shame when this or that part had to submit to be crushed by it. . . . He had, in acting, a keen sense of humour—of sardonic, grotesque, fantastic humour. He had an incomparable power for eeriness—for stirring a dim sense of mystery; and not less masterly was he in evoking a sharp sense of horror. His dignity was magnificent in purely philosophic or priestly gentleness, or in the gaunt aloofness of philosopher or king. . . . One felt that if Charles the Martyr, Dante, Wolsey, were not precisely as he was, so much the worse for Wolsey, Dante, Charles the Martyr. On the other hand, less august types, such as men of action and men of passion, were outside his range, and suffered badly when he dragged them into it.'

Though Irving 'could not do justice to the sound of blank verse, his primal appeal was always to the sense of beauty'—not obvious beauty but a 'strange, delicate, almost mystical and unearthly beauty'. Despite odd mannerisms of voice and gait 'Irving's presence dominated even those who could not be enchanted by it. His magnetism was intense, and unceasing . . . to it, rather than to the quality of his genius, which was a thing to be really appreciated only by the few, was due the unparalleled sway that he had over the many'.

Ellen Terry Ellen Terry, as an actress, is an enigma. Excepting only Mrs Siddons, no actress has left a more abiding legend; not one has left a legend more intangible. Some part of what she was like as a woman emerges from the letters to Shaw; we see, in brief, that she had brains as well as beauty. A photograph or two abundantly confirm her beauty when she was young and when she was in her prime; equally haunting photographs of her in old age hint at more, much more. (Were there no dark corners in that temple of luminosity?) Her beauty and her charm fed men's dreams and made lovers of her critics; their eulogies read more like rhapsodical valentines than dramatic criticism. The major devotee of the anti-pedestal brigade, Bernard Shaw . . . puts her on a pedestal! He tries to sing her praises in terms of the new thought, but it's palpably a case of the old feeling. He tries to

(1) Aged eight, as Puck (sitting on a
mechanical mushroom) in Charles Kean's
Midsummer Night's Dream, 1856

(2) Aged eighteen, 1866

her mid-thirties, as Beatrice in *Much Ado about Nothing*,

(4) Just before her eightieth birthday, from a photograph
by A. Warren published *Illustrated London News*, 1928.
(*Author's collection*)

make a New Woman of her; what happens is that she makes an old Romantic of him. (The treasured letters protest, protest that he will not sully the beauty of their letter-box-love by actually meeting her but, attitudinize as he will, we sniff something more than an elegant mockery of romance in this game of seek and hide.) The whole world it seems, was in love with her, new school and old alike; but lovers are not the most observant of critics and, though they all add proof upon proof of the magic she exerted, no clear definition of its alchemy emerges. What was it that she did with her charm, her brains and beauty that made her not only a lovely and lovable woman but a great actress? Enter enigma; and a few odd snippets of evidence.

'Miss Ellen Terry, whose keenness of intelligence is beyond all dissimulation, has often succeeded in making eminent critics believe that her stage-craft and nervous athleticism are mere efflorescences of her personal charm.' Stage-craft we understand readily enough; she had learnt her job from childhood onwards and knew how to project her subtlest thoughts to the back row of the gallery in the huge Lyceum theatre. But what does G.B.S. mean by nervous athleticism, a phrase he used more than once? Archer gives us a clue when he praises her 'intensity'; Winter gives us another: 'Miss Terry's acting has less mind in it than that of Mr Irving, though not deficient here, but it proceeds essentially from the nervous system—from the soul.' She appears, on occasion, to have abandoned herself to theatric excitement and Montgomery says that this could result in 'restless and aimless action, superfluity of gesture'. G.B.S. praises her when she later learned to control 'the mere brute force of tears and grief, which Miss Terry formerly employed so unscrupulously . . . that she made the audience positively howl with anguish. She now plays these scenes with infinite mercy and art, the effect, though less hysterical, being deeper'. This was apropos her playing in domestic drama and Comyns Carr confirms her success as Olivia in the dramatization of Goldsmith's *Vicar of Wakefield*. 'A creation of faultless taste and charm, so simple in its method, and so convincing in its reality, that even the most accomplished of those who played with her seemed to expose themselves to the reproach of artifice and convention.' Higher tragedy she seems not to have completely mastered—a tender, fragile Ophelia was within her compass but not Lady Macbeth. It is in high comedy that she excels—as Beatrice in *Much Ado About Nothing* and as Portia.

In the twenty-four years she spent as partner to Irving in the Lyceum company, much of the programme was devoted to stagey dramas, full of conventional situations and hackneyed sentiments. 'What shall be said of the personality that can make them fresh and new?' asks Winter, 'Miss Terry is spontaneous, unconventional and positively individual, and will use all characters in the drama for the expression of her own.' Montgomery adds to this 'Miss Terry is entirely original . . . she sees things as others might not see them, and she does things as others would not do them,' and praises her 'bright, fresh mind, her fluent vitality . . . her striking presence, her soft and musical voice.' Comyns Carr sums up: 'There is no actress of our time who can express with equal force or refinement the tenderness of a simple nature, the pathos that belongs to suffering that is past, or the playful gaiety of a sensitive temperament where laughter may quickly change to tears. . . . The most fortunate moments of her acting come so near to the magic of nature, the charm that she exerts at such times seems to be so completely the outcome of sudden inspiration, that

THE BRITISH
THEATRE

there is a danger of altogether ignoring the presence of an artistic faculty which is exercised with so much subtlety and finesse.' The restless sparkle of her temperament is echoed in her favourite quotation for autograph albums: 'A star danced, and under that I was born.'

Forbes-Robertson One more actor, Forbes-Robertson, must be mentioned. Not one of the great actors has made 'Hamlet' so much their own. We can still hear his voice on the old cracked record and marvel at his simplicity, the absence of the fustian we would have expected of his times—and have known in our own. Shaw records a decently restored text (Forbes-Robertson had learnt more than his splendid elocution from Phelps). 'The story of the play was perfectly intelligible, and quite took the attention of the audience off the principal actor at moments.' (The theatre was the Lyceum and this is the first of many gibes at Irving's otherly methods.) 'Instead of cutting every line that can possibly be spared, he retains every gem, in his own part or any one else's, that he can make time for in a spiritedly brisk performance. . . . He does not utter half a line; then stop to act; then go on with another half line; and then stop to act again, with the clock running away with Shakespear's chances all the time. He plays as Shakespear should be played, on the line and to the line, with the utterance and acting simultaneous, inseparable and in fact identical.' Shaw praises this Hamlet for 'seizing delightedly on every opportunity for a bit of philosophic discussion or artistic recreation to escape from the 'cursed spite' of revenge and love and other common troubles'—a true classical Hamlet who scorned 'the invariable resource of the instinctive, imaginative, romantic actor . . . weeping bucketsful of tears over Ophelia, and treating the players, the gravedigger, Horatio, Rosencrantz, and Guildenstern as if they were mutes at his own funeral'. Not a cold Hamlet, though: 'He is none of your logicians who reason their way through the world because they cannot feel their way through it: his intellect is the organ of his passion: his eternal self-criticism is as alive and thrilling as it can possibly be . . . . Mr Forbes-Robertson takes the part quite easily and spontaneously. There is none of that strange Lyceum intensity which comes from the perpetual struggle between Sir Henry Irving and Shakespear. The lines help Mr Forbes-Robertson at every turn, because he wants to play Hamlet, and not to slip into his inky cloak a changeling of quite another race . . . we get light, freedom, naturalness, credibility and Shakespear. It is wonderful how everything comes right when you have the right man with the right mind for it.' Because the actor does not superstitiously worship his author but enjoys him and understands his methods of expression, his 'performance has a continuous charm, interest and variety which are the result not only of his well-known grace and accomplishment as an actor, but of a genuine delight—the rarest thing on our stage—in Shakespear's art, and a natural familiarity with the plane of his imagination.' We are left thinking that this must have been the Hamlet of all Hamlets that we would most wish to see—and that we might well be surprised by the actor's modernity of outlook. His looks speak for themselves, classically handsome, both sensitive and strong; a voice of controlled beauty; a striking presence, the power that comes from repose. Actors thus lavishly endowed with superficial beauties usually lapse into romantic narcissism; this actor's mind and taste were too fastidious for that. He is a quite new kind of actor; the first of the many who were to bring a civilized approach into the jungle they inherited.

Forbes-Robertson as Hamlet. (*A photograph by Downeys*)

(1) As Hamlet, from a drawing by Gullick, 1897, in *Farewell Souvenir*

(2) As the Stranger in *The Passing of the Third Floor Back*, from a photograph by Caswell Smith in *Farewell Souvenir*

Forbes-Robertson

(3) As Caesar in Shaw's *Caesar and Cleopatra*. (*Rotary Photo Company*)

(4) As Shylock, from a photograph by J. Beagles & Co.

Oscar Wilde 'Enough is *not* as good as a feast.' The theatre of the nineties saw the coming of one more major figure—a writer who, like Shaw (and Chesterton, in other fields), found delight in paradox. Oscar Wilde's comedies of manners, *Lady Windermere's Fan*, *A Woman of No Importance* and *An Ideal Husband*, brought him great success and huge renown as a master of epigrammatic wit. Now, despite their sporadic brilliance, we see that they are, in the strictest sense, no more than 'prentice pieces. Wilde's elegant mother-wit bedded down with too conservative a mate—and the result was a litter of awkward mongrel pups, whose bad points draw disproportionate ridicule upon the good. The brilliant epigrams crackle intermittently but are made to appear strained in the mouths of characters made inappropriately subservient to the romantic theatre's fashion for crude melodramatic plots and hollow sentiments. Yet the town was well content and clamoured for more. Oscar the artist faced a trial perhaps even more packed with hubristic temptations than that which so tragically broke Oscar the man. Success always looks like a friend but can often prove an enemy. Oscar was dangerously susceptible to the flattery of success, dangerously deep-ingrained with narcissism, dangerously devoted to an unscrupulous hedonism. It seemed long odds against his finding the scrupulous pertinacity that was essential if he was not to drift with the tide and give the town what they would so obviously have been contented with—the mixture as before. But this was the trial that Oscar won. It is a triumphant victory against cruelly heavy odds. And one that we can take comfort in remembering when we are rightly harassed by the bitter memory of the trial that he (and everyone) lost.

Oscar Wilde—from a photograph by Ellis and Walery. (*Courtesy of London Electrotype Agency*)

Oscar Wilde at work—a caricature by Aubrey Beardsley

(1) **A scene from 'A Woman of no Importance'**—reproduced from *Illustrated London News*, 1893—showing Wilde's work very much under the influence of romantic melodrama that dominated the Theatre at the time he came into it. (*Copyright Illustrated London News*)

(2) **A scene from 'The Importance of being Earnest'.** Gwen Frangcon-Davies, Sir John Gielgud and Dame Edith Evans in Gielgud's revival of the play at the Phoenix Theatre, 1942. (*Copyright John Vickers*)

The creatures of Wilde's imagination could no more inhabit the play-modes of his times than Oscar himself could live by Marquess of Queensberry rules. He already had a mastery over the way he wanted his characters to talk. What he needed was to find a way of matching what they said and the way they said it to what they did and the way they did it; to be able to invent a sympathetic never-never land for them to inhabit that was as delicately poised in fantasy as both; and then to be able to keep each and every element in perfect accord with the others. This he did in *The Importance of Being Earnest* and the result is one entire and perfect chrysolite, wholly and utterly consistent with itself. As much of human nature as may properly emerge into high society is parodied in an elegant fantasy. Farce is the proper convention for people who speak as Wilde's characters do, for here we are never teased by the irrelevance of any considerations as to their reality. What had often seemed a brittle shallowness in the previous plays became revealed as a tempered delicacy in this. An elegant farce is a rare bird; there had not been anything quite like it before—and there has not been since. (Farce has only become a pejorative word because present day audiences associate it with the commercial drabberies—*Rixor Mortis*—to which the genre has lately fallen prey. Perhaps the more anarchic of our jesters will soon rescue it.)

For Oscar Wilde to have written the three early comedies was not difficult—was, in fact, dangerously easy. For Oscar, being Oscar, to have written *The Importance of Being Earnest* when the town would have been well content with *Lady Bracknell's Fan*, was a triumph—a feat to set the heart crowing.

Conclusion The century comes to an end with the renaissance well under way. The new drama of reform has opened its campaign and it has found disciples and a hearing, if not yet a universal welcome. The glitter of the old romances has been exposed as tinsel-stuff and the ground is at any rate partially cleared for any new master builders that may come along. The actors, too, have caught up—enough of them. They are learning that intelligence is not a bad companion to put alongside the nervous impromptu that was called emotional acting; they are learning that to play as a group with a unity of purpose can be as rewarding as jostling for the limelight; best of all, they are learning to serve their authors instead of mutilating them into their own service. Moreover, however heavily commercialized the general theatre may be, an audience is being found for plays with a minority appeal, some at least of which later find a favourable reception from larger audiences. This is a rosy picture; the fact that nine-tenths of the plays are still rubbishy romances (and nine-tenths of the actors still employed in pursuits that are crude, greedy or trivial) need deter only the more romantically pessimistic from looking forward with hope to the new century.

CHAPTER NINE

Twentieth Century Theatre - A Progress

'Dick, old chap, not another word about that money. Not a man of us but would have done just as you did, Heaven help us, if we got the chance. You were tempted, and you fell. . . . You have sinned; but you have suffered; and it was love that led you astray. Let the cold world say what it will, you shall have a happy ending, Dick, dear old man. God bless you. . . Go and live happily ever after. It's unmanly to—dash it, I think I'll go and smoke a pipe outside, if you don't mind, Dick.' Ibsen, says Shaw, 'might have been a rich man today if he had only taken that view of things. Perhaps, however, it is only fair that it should bring dramatic authors money; for it will assuredly not bring them anything else'.

The twentieth century theatre is distinguished by the number of men who wrote and worked for reasons other than money. Some of them may have, incidentally, made money (Shaw did) but it was not what they were after. The dramatists wrote out of an urgent good-neighbourliness, a blazing conviction that what they had to say was for the good of man. When their first plays failed—and they not only got no money for their pains but were also reviled by most of society and called 'Heretic!' (or worse)—they did not turn to writing the sort of plays that society seemed to want. They went on writing the sort of plays that they thought society needed, careless of what deprivations of money or social comfort their zeal might bring upon them.

Let's have no nonsense about the theatre dying. When its parade of altruists includes such giants as Ibsen, Shaw and Chekhov at the head of the hunger march, and such an impressive crowd of liberators following (all splendidly out of step), it is not of funerals that we must talk but of the baptism of fire. Church congregations have dwindled; politicians are losing their grip; and the old theatre (Dick's theatre) is dying, however it stretches out its death-scene. The new theatre has been born (and is growing)—'the greater Church' as Shaw calls it, which takes itself 'seriously as a factory of thought, a prompter of

155

Bernard Shaw at rehearsal

A sketch of G. B. S. at the rehearsal of *Arms and the Man* (1894) by Bernard Partridge (Gould), who played Saranoff. (*Author's collection*)

conscience, an elucidator of social conduct, an armoury against despair and dullness, and a temple of the Ascent of Man'. Dick, we may be sure, will look after himself (and his theatre). We have not time.

The Independent Theatre (founded by J. T. Grein) had presented, back in the early nineties, Ibsen's *Ghosts* as its first play and, during the next year, Shaw's first play, *Widower's Houses*, as part of its policy 'to give special performances of plays which have a literary and artistic rather than a commercial value'. The plays were presented for a bare few performances (often for a single matinée) and, in the early days of the movement, the performances were seldom available to the general public, attendance being limited to a small membership, not all of whom always let their enthusiasm deter them from leaving before the performance was completed. From such small beginnings, the movement grew until, some fifty years later during the latter years of the Hitler War, the State and private altruism combined to subsidize an independent Council to encourage with financial aid such theatre organizations as were prepared to set an artistic example to the commercial theatre. Now anyone who wants to take his mind and an inquiring spirit into the theatre can take his choice from a number of plays which will exercise both.

Bernard Shaw Ibsen's critics had seen to it that the popular mind thought of the reform plays as gloomy; Shaw set about changing all that. In the new Church of the theatre, he said 'the oftener you laugh the better, because by laughter only can you destroy evil without malice, and affirm good-fellowship without mawkishness'. Shaw learnt much of his way with an audience from his early experiences in street-corner oratory; here he had found that Saint George's wisdom only got a hearing if leavened with plenty of jokes from Joey the Clown. However he might protest that no Englishman would believe that you had a head unless you woke him up by standing on it, this is only a partial truth; it is made more complete by recognizing that Shaw just loved showing-off and would go to any lengths for applause. It is one of the strange paradoxes of his character that, though he displayed a superb nobility in never pandering to his audience and continued unswervingly to champion reform after unpopular reform, he nevertheless persisted in the base vulgarity of low prat-falls in the middle of high philosophy.

Shaw's critics protested that the theatre was no appropriate place to set up a pulpit for social reform. Shaw made no bones about the fact that he saw the theatre only as the best means of converting people to his view of life: 'I have no other object in writing plays.' The huge audiences that have flocked (and are still flocking) to the conversion meetings have forced the critics to change their minds, and the stage has been liberated for the social reform play. His critics protested that what he wrote were not plays but discussion-pieces and that his people were not real. Shaw admitted that his characters 'say not what in real life they could never bring themselves to say, even if they understood themselves clearly enough'; instead he makes them speak as if they were clever and honest enough to reveal their naked secret truths. It was a new way of laying bare a character's soul, as the 'aside' had done for centuries. Once the audience had familiarized itself with the new convention, it accepted it quite happily. It accepted also another novelty—that it was appropriate for a play to place an examination and discussion to follow a crisis; it recognized that this was

G. B. S. strikes out, Granville-Barker defends himself and Lillah McCarthy intervenes—a scene from a rehearsal of *Androcles and the Lion*

G. B. S. in later years, from a photograph in *Bernard Shaw through the Camera*

(1) **St Joan.** Sybil Thorndike as St Joan kneels to pray in the Cathedral. Scene designed by Charles Ricketts 1924

(2) **The Apple Cart.** Scene designed by Paul Shelving 1929

(3) **Don Juan in Hell.** Alec Clunes as Don Juan in the Arts Theatre production, 1952 (settings by Fanny Taylor). (*Copyright Angus McBean*)

just what happened at home. The stage had been liberated for the discussion play. Shaw's critics protested that his plays were all talk, lacked action and plot, clever but without heart. (The old fallacy that to have a mind forbids you having a feeling heart dies hard.) They saw action as a series of sensational attempts at felony, would not believe that a play had a plot unless they could see the bones sticking well out through the flesh, and preferred the mawkish sentiments of hearts worn on sleeves to Shaw's disturbing concern that all his fellow creatures (even those that 'sat below the salt') should share as much of equal opportunity as society could be organized to provide for them. Shaw's training and bent was musical; he saw the pattern of his plays in symphonic terms and their dialogue in terms of musical rhetoric; a technique which gave a firm but unobtrusive structure and a flavour of excitement to his intellectual examination and discussion.

Shaw took what people thought was real (or desirable) and turned it not so much topsy-turvy as inside-out. An up to date, informed and commonsensical, teasing fellow is put in among the relics to help the play expose them for what they really are, romantic shams. The fashionable musical-comedy plot and setting yield to *Arms and the Man*, the fashionable melodrama plot and setting yield to *The Devil's Disciple*. The unfashionable but topical *A Doll's House* sees woman as the doll in the house, *Candida* sees man as the doll. The nineties saw man as The Tempter and woman as The Frail Sex; *Man and Superman* sees man as frail and woman as the tempter, though in the new Eden she looks not forward to the tree of knowledge but backward to old nesting habits. And so on . . . inside look out, outside look in.

Shaw's value to the theatre was not so much that he introduced it to liberating technical reforms but that he reminded it that it must never forget its purity of purpose. His value to the community was to give a momentum to reform which would have moved much slower but for this most challenging and amusingly provocative voice.

Strindberg Not even the warmest admirer of the next reformer would claim that he was amusing. If Shaw saw woman as an enemy to the higher disciples of the life force, he challenged her with knightly good humour and gallantry. Strindberg (whose home life was so different from that of our dear George) fought with all the savage desperation of a trapped creature. Strindberg is less known, more misrepresented and less respected than he should be—we still let the old blanket-denigration of 'Scandinavian gloom' obscure the Northern Lights. As with Ibsen, the more you get to know Strindberg, the more you find in the plays. The specious image of a pathological woman-hater soon evaporates. *The Father* (the only one of his plays with which we have been able to gain more than a fleeting familiarity) soon ceases to be about a fanatic crank who sees all women as monsters and becomes a very real warning that a man had better never let over-caring make him a doll in his own house. The play is alive today, much of its work still undone; it is ripe for revival, for example, in America, where the malaise of an obsessive matriarchy is still putting too many men in straitjackets to the tune of old childhood lullabies.

When the first anti-Strindberg critics set up their Freudian yelping, introspection and self-analysis were still suspect heresies; now that these are more commonplace, the plays may seem less suspect. What *is* gloomy is that we don't see more of the plays more often;

Strindberg, by Albert Bonnier. (*Courtesy of Mrs M. Holtermann*)

Anton Chekhov. (*Copyright Theatre Collection, New York Public Library*)

they are, in many respects, newer than many more recent plays. Strindberg was not only one of the first writers who might be called post-Freudian but remains one of the few who have written plays from that angle of vantage. Meanwhile, students of dramatic form can examine the technical mysteries from the printed plays. It is not only an attitude of mind that gives the plays their intensity, but a technical skill in condensation, a nervous compression. If we examine a short scene whose pace appears to be no more than that of reality, we find that the characters pack whole months of progression into its short minutes. It is a succession of such scenes that gives the plays their feeling of violence. Accept the convention (as we do many less acceptable) and the plays reveal a psychological depth of truth that far exceeds the more superficial realities.

The Father is, more or less, in the Ibsen manner of *A Doll's House* (and like Shaw's *Candida* sees the man as the doll). In his later plays, Strindberg, as Ibsen had done, sought to enlarge the frontiers of drama beyond such comparative naturalism. In the early years of the century Freud and his disciples were seeking to understand and cure the abnormalities of temporarily unbalanced minds by studying minds more permanently abnormal, to whom daydreams and nightmares were their whole life. Both Ibsen and Strindberg, in their later plays, wrote poems on such themes, dream plays haunted by expressive symbolism. This is such an unfamiliar use of the theatre, and we are still so inescapably part of a climate that resists such extremes of unfamiliarity in plays, that the time has not even yet come when we can make up our minds with any certainty as to how valid such assays might prove. There are growing and welcome signs that we may be given the opportunity. Meanwhile, even such limited knowledge as we have of them has exerted an influence that has helped later dramatists to push out still further beyond the barriers of naturalism.

161

Chekhov It is evening time and the spent leaves fall. Autumn has come and the old feudal world is dying. Hearts are breaking and shoe-strings are broken—the people flit like dazed butterflies and trip like near-sighted clowns. It is the hush before the storm of revolt and reform. And the music that Chekhov makes of it, strains compassion to its tenderest limits. Easy enough to have compassion for the poor; hard, very hard for us now to have compassion for those who let riches leave them thus enervated and irresponsible. Yet the senses ache as the muted apology is made—and the grim warning given.

The inhabitants of 'the country houses of Europe were the only repositories of culture who had social opportunities of contact with our politicians, administrators, and newspaper proprietors, or any chance of sharing or influencing their activities. But they shrank from that contact. They hated politics. They did not wish to realize Utopia for the common people; they wished to realize their favourite fictions and poems in their own lives; and, when they could, they lived without scruple on incomes which they did nothing to earn. . . . Even in private life, they were often helpless wasters of their inheritance . . . even those who lived within their incomes were really kept going by their solicitors and agents, being unable to manage an estate or run a business without continual prompting from those who have to learn how to do such things or starve'. Shaw describes Chekhov's people—and then their tragedy: 'Nature demoralizes us with long credits and reckless overdrafts, and then pulls us up cruelly with catastrophic bankruptcies.' At least four of Chekhov's plays are masterpieces on this theme, the swan-songs of a dying world, the preludes to the Russian revolution that came fourteen years after Chekhov had left us in an empty country house, while outside in the orchard the axe began to level all to the ground.

'Time will pass, and we shall go away for ever, and we shall be forgotten, our voices, and how many there were of us; but our sufferings will pass into joy for those who will live after us, happiness and peace will be established upon earth, and they will remember kindly and bless those who lived before. . . .' As Chekhov's music plays, our tears are compulsory. But we may well ask . . . for what? Is it only for the beauty of the music, the delicate requiem for romance that must die? The music is so persistent, so hypnotic, and our senses are so tuned to let it make us slaves to it alone, that there is grave danger of letting it lull the mind to rest. It is the unshed tears of the mind that haunt our spirits; and here their source lies in a compassionate irony. This is demanded for the fatuous inadequacy of these frail fellow-creatures who are so busy crying for a losing past that they cannot answer the future's desperate call for a winning present.

'Ten or fifteen years ago there were six big country houses round the shore. It was all laughter, and noise, and the firing of guns, and love-making, love-making without end.' If we only hear the lilt of the Last Waltz in that love-making, love-making, shall we ever learn the secret of the Lost Chord? When, at the end of *The Cherry Orchard*, the long threnody for muted strings falters at last, what is it that we hear as the harsh percussion of the axe shocks us into sense? Only an old world of illusion dying? Only a new world of illusion in the making? Both? Or more?

The student of technique may find in Ibsen and Strindberg a mastery of compression; in Chekhov a mastery of protraction. They condense months into pertinent days; each sentence is packed tight, spare and telling; even the allegorical upper storey is compact.

Above UNCLE VANYA—The Moscow Arts Theatre Setting for Stanislawsky's production, 1899
Below THE SEAGULL—Komisarjevsky's setting for his production in London, 1936

Chekhov stretches his evenings until they seem like months; his sentences yearn into elaborate melodies; but his allegory is no part of the building but free as the sky. He makes his silences speak more than his words, his words prompt other thoughts than those they state. It is another use of what the Freudians were working on, the revelation of the inner mysteries of character by seeing the outer commonplace utterances as defence mechanisms, armour. Chekhov makes psychiatrists of us all as we read between the lines; but he imposes few limits of definition on what he challenges us to find there for ourselves. In his theatre, each auditor is set free to write his own allegory, choose his own hauntings. It is a cunning defence against romantic acting and play-going; the illusionists may indulge themselves but they will not outwit his greater magic. He liberates the stage from those who wanted everything done for them in a play and welcomes audience participation at the highest level, one that must provide its own constant counterpoint to his melodic theme.

Pirandello A man is at the centre of a circle of friends and acquaintances. He sees himself one way; they see him each in a different way. The sum-total of what they see as being him will be quite different from his own idea of himself. How can you be sure that your own idea of yourself is more 'real' than their idea of you? How much more are you than the sum of your world's varied reactions to you? (If you regard the theory as totally invalid, try and get your mother, your wife and your child to see how much they agree about your character and then see how it compares with your own observations.) Pirandello was a disciple of this school of relativity and his plays evolve a number of exercises on the theme. The theory is a frightening one; carried to its logical extreme it sets you questioning whether you exist at

Luigi Pirandello

This caricature was the frontispiece to his book, *Vieille Sicile*, 1928

all except as a series of reactions to your surroundings; small wonder that when Pirandello introduced his critics to it, they sought to mitigate their fear by proclaiming that even if the theme might have a strictly relative validity, the plays certainly had no place in a theatre. 'Cerebral', they said (and say), flinging the word over their shoulder as they beat a ruffled retreat. To which we can now say 'What of it?' The theatre is there to illumine the spirit of man and there are more doors than one into that house of mystery; you are as liable to get in through the one labelled 'mind' as through the one labelled 'senses'. (Though they don't look all that different to some of us—the door is there and it's quicker to open it than hang about reading (or making) false labels.)

We all have our favourite books and our favourite characters in them. Hamlet is more real than my young friend who has just come down from university, and Falstaff more real than my fat friend in the pub next door—relatively speaking. Pirandello peoples his stage-within-a-stage with six characters in search of an author who has denied them life because he has discontinued writing their play (which had the germs of truth in it) in order to proceed with a sentimental romantic play for which an audience is always waiting. The characters insist on living out their own play, based on the true 'reasons, one crueller and viler than the other, that have made this of me', revealing their nausea for the romantic story to which the audience is turning as the curtain finally falls. The parable is a vivid plea for realities deeper than naturalism and for the acceptance of a new convention in which to see a play. Each successive revival of *Six Characters* has shown audiences increasingly eager to respond. The only other play which is at all well-known in this country, *Henry IV*, is such a forbidding visitor that it puts the clock back for Pirandello each time it is played; we drop

Sean O'Casey, extracted from a photo of the O'Caseys, frontispiece to *Sunset and Evening Star*, Macmillan 1954. (*Courtesy of Sean O'Casey*)

The Silver Tassie

Scene for Act Two at the Apollo, 1929, by Augustus John. (*Copyright executors of Augustus John and Mander and Mitchenson Theatre Collection*)

it a formal intellectual curtsey and refrain from looking it in the eyes. Having deferred, we defer. There are many other plays, and, from what can be guessed by miserably random reading, they deserve to be allowed to challenge us in a theatre. Many have not been introduced to us in this country even in print.

Ibsen, Strindberg, Shaw and Chekhov all put the allegory upstairs and kept the ground floor 'real' (to one extent or another). Pirandello puts the allegory firmly on the ground floor and leaves us to seek the reality upstairs. Whether or no we are ready to accept his constant theme, whether or no we think the plays belong less to the theatre than to the study, any student will find that Pirandello has few rivals in technical virtuosity.

Ibsen, Shaw, Strindberg, Chekhov, Pirandello. They came as liberators; and stayed for the occupation, benevolent despots who were welcome when we saw that they were not only demolition contractors but master builders. Convinced of their altruism, we allow them to tax us; and find them the best of good neighbours. They deserve at least a statue and many days of remembrance. No National Theatre's (surely international) programme will be complete without them. We cannot be so sure of the innovators that have followed them —many may be of equal stature, but they stand too close for us to be able to get them into perspective. When you try to look at something under your nose, you squint. What is needed is a bird's-eye-view; all that is available is a worm's-eye-view. Final superlatives, then, had better be left for later chroniclers. This one will be content to name some of the runners in the race and let time decide who wins in the long run.

The New Writers Hitherto, dialect had been used only for minor characters, usually comic. Synge saw the theatre of the mind as joyless. He and O'Casey used the joyful rhythms of

Irish speech to show that dialect could reveal more than it obscured. We have learnt our lesson so well that, judging by the current decade of television plays, we are now in danger of believing that nothing can be real unless it is in dialect. The Irishmen's plays are sound at heart and we belittle them when we only accept them at their charming face value.

The Americans (you could say) speak our language; it is not unnatural that we have each come to know the other's drama. Too much of this neighbourliness has been a matter of taking in each other's dirty washing; but some more proper gift-parcels have been exchanged from time to time. No visitor to America should travel without one of those handy little brochures about how to get on with the natives. The proud display of so many archaic relics (like the guard that never changes its love of protection-money; the mammoth overheated conservatories; and all those Buck Palaces) gives this backward, decadent and insular old country a certain quaint old-world charm for those of us who come from Europe's younger civilizations. But we must be careful, as we squander our new riches of the mind, not to give the tactless impression that we own the joint, or to breach any of those fascinating formal etiquettes that surround the reigning monarchy of mammon. And to honour those who have dared to break with the mummifying traditions.

Eugene O'Neill has earned our respect for the bravery of his opposition to the confining influences of fashion in both social attitudes and theatrical forms. The Old Country owes much to this versatile disciple of our New World. An ex-sailor, he is the Drake of his times, the most skilled and courageous of pirates, a mass-importer, for ever plundering our richest cargoes. Realism, expressionism, Freudianism, impressionism, relativism—Europe makes 'em and he takes 'em. And makes of them rich challenges to the American theatre's poverty of imagination and aristocracy of philistinism. A truly admirable man, the founder of the American altruistic theatre; a big statue on a very small building. Clifford Odets has a statue there, too; but it is crumbling fast. They are still waiting for Lefty, singing but not awake; the golden boy turned gilty and went off to the lost paradise of Hollywood, too small an end for such a big beginning. The poet Macleish invaded the new theatre of radio; his *Fall of the City* is one of the very few memorable and abiding masterpieces in a medium devoted too exclusively to ephemeral slave-pieces. If it had not been written in the alien and suspect tongue of poetry, more Americans might have heard its warning. As it is, we are forced to ask—need the Amercian theatre be such a *hell* of a *business*? Too much of the water around its shores still reeks of the spilt hooch of prohibitionism; what it needs is another Boston tea-party. The new satirists are sending out invitations. Not too many of them are arrested. There is always hope.

From our distant cousins to our nearer neighbours—France. Out of the nineties came a play that sent all the trappings of romanticism tripping over its hero's long nose. *Cyrano* is even harder to get close to than most French plays because Rostand's verse, alas, defies translation. All that we have heard (or can read) of him in English emerges as mere jingle-jangle and provokes the same disrespectful laughter as an opera libretto read in cold blood. Not even this can hide from us that Cyrano Long-Nose is of the stuff from which legends are made, a minor Quixote in a major drama, one of the earliest and tallest of the anti-heroes, a prodnose among the litter-louts. Out of the nineties, too, came the Belgian Maeterlinck. Chekhov's slowing down of tempo has been noted; James Agate saw the characters as 'fixed

Eugene O'Neill
(Copyright Brugiere Collection, New York Public Library)

All God's Chillun' Got Wings
The London Production with Paul Robeson and Flora Robson 1933
(Courtesy of George Freedley)

in time almost as a photograph is fixed'. If Chekhov brings the family album to life, Maeterlinck's even more static theatre brings the close-up to life. Nothing, it seems, could be slower than *The Interior*. One or two neighbours stand in long-drawn hesitation outside the windows of a household still secure in the frail trivia of day-to-day contentment, still happily unaware of the tragic news that the visitors cannot bring themselves to break. Which speaks closer to us, the muted undertones outside or the unspoken living that the windows cannot veil? It is a minor masterpiece, simple and direct, a slow movement quick with life. Maeterlinck was best known here for his long fantasy for children, the whimsy-whamsy *Blue Bird*. Now that we've forgotten that, the short *Interior* and some other pieces in the same vein would be found well worth our time in the theatre of today.

Jean-Jacques Bernard came in the twenties to teach us what he had learnt from Chekhov. His plays are deceptively slight (though agreeably delicate) when read; but when properly acted they have one uncommon power. The character says one thing; we hear another—what he is thinking. No one has had greater ability than this Freud-in-the-theatre to make us hear the unspoken 'aside' of a character's thoughts and feelings. Alas, the magic of this technical sleight-of-hand is often performed with objects a little too light-weight. Giraudoux asked us to look again at fantasy, the stuff of the old fairy stories and folk-legends. To these he lent much grace and some purpose. Anouilh followed to play Grimm to his Hans Andersen, his more modern fantasies haunted by dark as well as light ghosts, more substantial but easier to see through. The existentialists advertised a stimulating but not very complex creed that explored the paradoxical irony of rational man stubbing his toes on the irrational and the anti-rational. Sartre saw this as hell and himself as a dark devil; neither the creed's portentous name nor Sartre's (wonderfully dramatic) hoof-beating and horn-wagging need impose similar melodramatic limitations on a surrealist theme that the theatre might find better suited, as many painters have done, to wry comedy.

Sort of half-French, half-Irish is Beckett, whose *Waiting for Godot* set the revolutionary cat among the romantic pigeons with a vengeance. Critics have tried to persuade us that Sartre sees us as all in hell and Beckett as all up to the neck in dustbins. And so, of course, we are; and it's all very tragic and very funny. Now that heaven, earth and hell have grown to be next-door-neighbours (not even semi-detached), and are fixed at each and every moment of time, Godot waits for no man—and least of all for the sluggish spirits who seek to escape to sad crumbling fun-fairs, muttering incantations like 'gloomy' instead of finding glory in the urgent adventure that the new proximity and imminence evoke.

'The comic is the unusual, pure and simple; nothing surprises more than banality; the "sur-real" is there, within our reach, in our daily conversation.' When words are worn out, as Ionesco sees our world, such material platitudes as chairs and coffee-cups assume a domination, multiplying till they hide and reveal the uninhibited people. Man cannot live by chairs and coffee-cups alone. Unless we use our loaf, our daily bread (and our dough) will swell till the spirit is edged out of the room. No one can call Ionesco 'gloomy'; he is magnificent fun—and, like all great clowns, has a proper command over anguish. He comes from an occupied country, Rumania, but has found a home in France—and the beginnings of a welcome (which must swell) in our own country.

And so to home. Is T. S. Eliot English or American? Born there, like so many of their   169

Samuel Beckett—*Trends in Twentieth Century Drama*, by Lumley Rockliffe

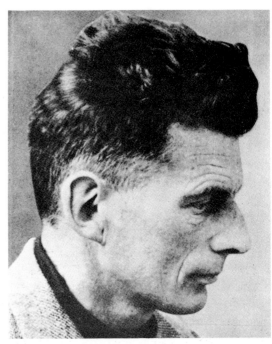

Waiting for Godot, Arts Theatre, 1955. (*Copyright Houston-Rogers*)

S. Eliot. (*Copyright Camera Press Ltd*)

Christopher Fry. (*Copyright Peter Neville Ltd*)

artists he has followed the compulsion to feel the fresher winds of Europe, perhaps discomforted by houses too preoccupied with 'the hot' and 'putting the heat on'. A cool poet, severe and straight, his *Murder in the Cathedral*, when it came in the mid-thirties, showed at very long last that poetic drama could be freed from the rococo *appliqué* that had for centuries reduced plainsong to musical embroidery. Auden and Isherwood, for a while, spoke freshly for poetry in the theatre; but went away when not enough of us found time to listen. Better still, Louis MacNeice unclogged the ether with a succession of radio dramas in verse that put to proper shame the niggard vocabulary of our sound radio.

The Hitler War left an aftermath of living on rationed food and with plain matchboard-thin homes and furniture; we were on short commons, reduced to the bare 'utilities'. Christopher Fry came along, singing with a welcome elaboration, offering all 'the convolutions of the convolvulus'. We crept out of the concrete and let his abstractions lead us back to play-time. No one born since can feel as we did, crawling out of dark shelters, the breathtaking wonder of that release into the light. Later plays have found him strangely ashamed of his exuberance and fun, pruning his verse hard back. Denying us these, he seems like a man who had wilfully tied one hand behind his back under the impression that it will strengthen the other. The comic and the tragic made such a good match of it in *The Lady's Not For Burning* and *Venus Observed*; it seems a pity to drive them to divorce. Is Fry going to devote his autumn wholly to bare branches, must we lose the sacred sound of his laughter? We are still at war.

171

12*

The Lady's Not for Burning

Oliver Messel's design for John Gielgud's production, 1949

The world was almost taken prisoner. While might is still allowed its wrongful rights, it can happen again. Bridget Boland's *The Prisoner* dramatized the battle for the mind between prisoner and captor (a sort of faith and a sort of science). Each are brain-washed to naked exhaustion; forced company becomes desired companionship; when 'freedom' comes to part them, we are left wondering which is the convert—and deploring that they must see themselves as separate. It is an epic theme; and Miss Boland is to be congratulated on her courage and on her perseverance. She moves ever further from challenge and ever nearer to conquest with each revision. The play has now been seen on stage, film and television; and each time we see it, it has gained in power.

Peter Ustinov, born and bred in England, but of mixed blood, is the first really cosmopolitan dramatist. He goes everywhere (and sees everything), retailing the wide world's foibles to us in a series of keen monologues. No after-dinner speaker is more welcome on our television screens, no impersonator more trenchantly accurate. There is not a sound, it seems, however alien or exotic, that his keen ear cannot record or his voice reproduce. Verbal mimicry is a country quite without frontiers for him, and he makes of us all the most eager fellow-travellers. He takes a very proper delight in showing-off these powers (there is nothing miserly about his helpings); and he plays this game in a variety of moods that range from the gentlest of admonitory teasing to the most savage and slashing attacks. The uninhibited brilliance is so dazzling that we are in danger of missing the Freudian ticks that reveal the inner humility and the compassion. An inhibited self-deprecatory snort often follows the good story superbly told, rather in the manner of a traveller needing to feel at one with stay-at-homes. Then vulnerable eyes peer from neighbour to neighbour anxiously seeking not applause but confirmation that, however outrageously his genius may have led

172

him to colour the telling, there has been no wounding beyond the bounds of a scrupulous justice. His comic plays are extensions of the monologues. *Romanoff and Juliet*, like so many of his stories, was so full of fantastic fun that it was easy to overlook how slyly he was educating us beyond our insularity to world-neighbourliness. Tragedy is a bird that he has flown at more often than he has caught—to his own chagrin (and our relief that there is *something* the prodigious fellow cannot master). His courageous altruism, we may be sure, will not be denied; though some of us may hope that he will find content in letting it continue to ride tandem with his wondering sense of fun.

The dividing line is 1955—*Waiting for Godot* is the play. Reading it in manuscript before it was performed, it was clear that it epitomized all that provokes philistine critics to hatred. One could already hear the massing of their biggest battalions, the tried and rusty defenders, the one touch of fear in nature that makes the whole world kin to Clement Scott—and less than humankind. A parrot with a good memory could have written the notices: 'Why do these arty pretentious highbrows dote so much on gloom and mystification, nothing happens there's no plot no action it's all talk and then you don't know what he means why doesn't he say what he means?' These killing little words had delayed our acceptance of every major dramatist of note since the nineties. Only five years before, the critics had flung them at John Whiting's *Saint's Day*, stinging our major dramatists, directors and actors to speak out in defence of what was palpably, at the very least, a major talent in the making. Beckett was nearly murdered in the very same cathedral, *Godot* provoked the same mad-bull spleen. With two exceptions, the new exceptions. Two critics stood out for the play—and the public went in thousands to judge for themselves. The day was won; and now only

PETER USTINOV, taking part in 'The Brains Trust', 4th February, 1960. (*Copyright British Broadcasting Corporation*)

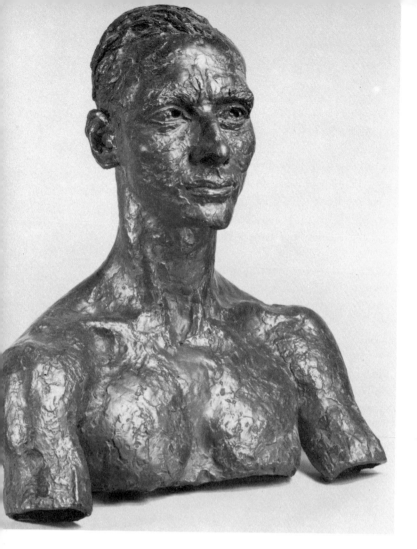

Mid-century actors

(1) SIR JOHN GIELGUD, from a bronze bust by Epstein. (*Author's collection*)

(2) SIR LAURENCE OLIVIER as Richard III, 1944. (*Copyright John Vickers*)

Dame Edith Evans as Lady Bracknell in *The Importance of Being Earnest.* (*Copyright J. Arthur Rank*)

Dame Sybil Thorndike as St Joan, 1924. (*Copyright Bertram Park*)

Bridget Boland, 'The Prisoner'. Sir Alec
Guinness and Noel Willman in a scene from the play,
1956. (*Copyright Angus McBean*)

Dylan Thomas, Under Milk Wood, 1956 designed by Michael
Tangmar. (*Copyright Angus McBean*)

the more obstinate witch-doctors mutter the old incantations. Since then a wealth of new ground has been cleared, and we all get a chance to join in the new fertility-rites.

This major break with the older traditions left Osborne, a young man of twenty-six, free to look back in anger on those responsible for the poverty of youth's inheritance. The glib label, 'angry young men', was used to seek to diminish their stature by reminding us that young men have always disrespected their elders. But there was a commanding maturity about the way that Osborne mirrored the justifications for youth's anger; he has helped to liberate the old-fashioned, less of whom now dare to say 'children should be seen and not heard'. The poet Dylan Thomas had written his *Under Milk Wood* as a radio play for voices. His evocative images sent skirts ballooning with the joyous disrespect of a high wind; and there were other private places that this fresh fellow left the better for his airs. Thomas made his words look new. Pinter came along and collected all the second-hand and antique words; the used words; and deployed them to illustrate the comedy and pathos of our lack of ability to make them communicate anything more than our isolation. Alun Owen, Henry Livings, John Mortimer, John Arden, Gwyn Thomas, Arnold Wesker, Giles Cooper are all free (to a certain extent) to expect that their experiments will find a reasonably enfranchised hearing from both critics and audience; and their abilities guarantee that our serious theatre-going can be adventurous and challenging.

Now that almost anything goes, is it valid to ask 'will anything stay?'

175

Bertolt Brecht. (*Copyright Camera Press*)

Brecht And so to Brecht and his 'battle for a theatre fit for a scientific age', the anti-heroic theatre with its creed of 'alienation'. In Brecht's plays the actor must not attempt to 'carry the audience with him . . . he must not hide the fact that he is performing—he must underline it and make it clear that he knows he is being observed'. He must, in fact, do the reverse of what Hitler did. And we, the audience, must remain unbewitched, the playgoer must not 'lose himself' in the play. We shall thus avoid the German Sin, the submission of a cultured people to the hypnosis of mad rhetoric. The creed seems to have no universal validity unless you believe that it is only through the senses that people can be duped, and that the mind is impregnable. In the battle against subservience to illusions, as many campaigns have to be fought against wrong thinking as against wrong feeling. Brecht died before he completed his contribution, somewhere midway in his exploration—we do him no justice to fossilize into laws the uncompleted thesis of a man always vitally (scientifically) open to change, always hideously (romantically) haunted by a fear of what horrors 'emotion' could betray people into.

The application of the theory of 'alienation' is, nevertheless, proving of immense value to the evolution of the theatre, crystallizing a growing mood for simpler staging and more truthful acting. One hopes that it is the final nail in the coffin of the actor whose self-indulgent irrelevant 'emoting' has obscured the truth of mind in both old and new plays; and that it is not to be made the corner-stone of any new thesis devoted to defining the theatre-with-a-mind as a theatre-without-senses. Our journey is not from senses-without-mind to mind-without-senses but to a proper integration of senses and mind. Any Brechtian who sees monochrome as revealing and colour as obscuring is half-way to being colour blind. The proper scientist is a man of spirit and blinks at nothing.

An Experimental Conclusion 'A theatre fit for a scientific age' might do well to take a leaf out of science's own text-book. (And that, in its random way, is exactly what it has been trying to do for the last seventy or so years.) The bogey-makers tell us that science is mere materialism, an impertinent attempt to discover the laws of nature; and try to dismiss the theatre in this scientific age as anarchic and unspiritual. The bogey-makers are, as usual, talking sensual non-sense. Science is not concerned with laws but with experiment; and experiments are the gestures of a man of spirit to the universal anarchy of infinity. Laws are fixed; but science sees that time and the world change and move; and that yesterday's law, the father's law, must always be out-of-date for today's son. Science starts each day afresh, knowing that however much it remembers from yesterday it may know nothing of today; probes till it finds a fact; refrains from relating that fact to any other fact until a re-lationship has been proved; and sets up no generalizations (or 'laws') from that proof. Where the pre-scientific mind sees laws and an attainable goal, science humbly sees only hints as to a direction for further re-search. It is content to move on to a point of arrival that must be as limited as time, space and thought are unlimited. It is thus, unlike superstitions and dogmas, continually open to correction, continually evolving, always seeking the most enterprising, least wasteful step nearer to an ever-changing unknown.

If you are so sadly subject to illusion as to see any one part of infinitude as final—and think that the Atom Bomb, for example, will destroy all life—do not let the bogey-makers tempt you to blame science for this primitive fear. All science has done (so far) is to provide the most efficient engine of destruction. Who drives the engine—and by whose permission? You drive it; or let someone else drive it for you; unless you face your responsibility to choose (scientifically) better rulers, to work for better social organization. If some of us die, it will be not because the atom bomb has been invented but because we have let ourselves be hoodwinked into thinking that there is truth in such hollow slogans as 'a life given in the service of one's country or one's god is a life well given'—(there's a *lazy law* for you, an arrogant blasphemy that would send the coolest scientist sobbing to his grave). The only giving is living. The only way is experiment. That it must be conscious and controlled experiment is a matter for re-search and search again, not for dogma's frozen laws.

Young science must stop taking bribes from old illusion's commerce; and put away its toys for the leisure-play of some future Guy Fawkes Night. There is adult's work to be done, a full day's work with well-paying overtime; urgent, top-priority, and no secret . . . mate. Is it really beyond the wit of science to make our States our servants instead of our masters; to experiment with one small exemplary society devoted to being good neighbours instead of bad, welcoming new diversities and despising old uniformities? Eager emigrants are waiting; not a little disgusted with the delay; but not without hope. As the old dogmas' sign-posts to unattainable utopias rot and slump to the ground, the theatre offers its mirrors, saying 'this is how you are' and provoking you to plan how you would be. It is an adult and contemporary gesture. Is it asking too much? Splitting the atom would be child's play to that.

How long, O Science, how long?

Twentieth Century Theatre—A Progress

177

Alec Clunes as Thomas Mendip in *The Lady's Not for Burning*, by Christopher Fry. (*Copyright Angus McBean*)

Index

Where page numbers are given in italics, thus, *158*, they refer to a caption.

Index

180